This Book Belongs To:

_____

_____

_____

Mychal Wynn
and
Dee Blassie

Rising Sun Publishing
Marietta, GA
(800) 524-2813

Mychal Wynn
and
Dee Blassie

Building Dreams®

Elementary School Edition

Teacher's Guide

Mychal Wynn is also the author of

Building Dreams: Helping Students Discover Their Potential (book, teacher/parent workbook, and audio tape)

Empowering African-American Males to Succeed: A Ten-Step Approach for Parents and Teachers (book, teacher/parent workbook, and audio tape)

Enough is Enough: The Explosion in Los Angeles

Don't Quit — Inspirational Poetry

The Eagles who Thought They were Chickens (book, teacher's guide, student activity book, and audio tape)

Dee Blassie is a classroom teacher with over 18 years of experience in elementary education who trains nationally on the material covered in this book.

To schedule parent training, staff development, or keynote presentations contact:

Rising Sun Publishing/Training and Staff Development

(800) 524-2813

FIRST EDITION 1995

Building Dreams®: Elementary School Edition Teacher's Guide

Copyright © 1995 by Rising Sun Publishing.

All rights reserved. Classroom teachers may reproduce limited quantities of the activities, sample letters and procedural charts for use in their individual classrooms. Copying for entire schools, and/or school districts, or use in curriculum programs is prohibited without expressed written permission from Rising Sun Publishing. Video and audio tapes, procedural charts, posters, and other support materials are available from Rising Sun Publishing.

No part of this book may be reproduced or transmitted in any form or by any means, electronic or mechanical, including photocopying, recording, or stored in any information storage and retrieval system for commercial purposes.

ISBN 1-880463-45-8

Rising Sun Publishing
P.O. Box 70906
Marietta, Georgia 30007-0906
(800) 524-2813

Printed in the United States of America.

Acknowledgments

We would like to acknowledge those teachers who are implementing many of the ideas and activities contained in this book. You will know who you are because you will find yourself reading this book and saying, "I do that," or "That's a great idea; I'm going to do that!" You will find yourself sharing the ideas and activities contained in this book with your colleagues to help them to help children better.

Mychal Wynn personally acknowledges the many gifted, talented, and caring elementary school teachers who have attended his training sessions and are developing wonderful classroom and school-wide activities to help children discover their dreams and aspirations. From Felton Laboratory School in Orangeburg, South Carolina, to Welborn Elementary School in Kansas City, Kansas, and the hundreds of schools in between, you have inspired me to continue as you have inspired our children to dream. I would also like to acknowledge my son's pre-kindergarten teacher Toni Douglas, and first grade teacher Barbara Mabary, who have helped him to build his dreams.

I would also like to acknowledge my editor, Denise Mitchell Smith of Los Angeles, who is always there, helping me to tap my potential.

Dedication

This book is dedicated to those professional educators who are always listening, learning, experimenting, growing, and taking risks to help children realize more of their limitless potential. Society doesn't pay you enough, respect you enough, or support you enough, yet you continue to teach when you could be doing other things to make more money, earn more respect, be better supported and appreciated.

Mychal Wynn dedicates this book to his best friend and wife, Nina, their sons Mychal-David and Jalani, and to those too many to name who have shared their kindness, inspiration, support, encouragement, knowledge, information, and prayers in helping him to achieve his dreams.

Dee Blassie dedicates this book to her husband, Tom, for his constant support, patience, and love so that she can pursue her dreams and to all the 24-hour teachers who have the influence to create the dreamers of tomorrow.

Dee also thanks her parents, Larry and Nellie VonderHaar; her sister, Debbie Sobeck, for encouraging her to be a dreamer; Rob Sainz, principal, Ginny Altrogge, assistant principal, and the staff at Carman Trails School in Parkway School District for allowing her the freedom to turn her dreams into a reality; and Audrey Jackson for introducing her to Mychal Wynn so that they could become a dream team. Finally a thumbs up to La Salle University for providing her with the opportunity to succeed.

Contents

About the Authors VIII
Introduction X
How to Use This Book XIII
Why should we Build Dreams? XVI

Teacher Assessment 1
Dream-Building School and Classroom Components 3

Activity 1	Pre-Assessment	6
Activity 2	Invitational Learning Leads to Bonding	12
Activity 3	Teacher Idea Board/Activity Book	20

Preparing Your Classroom

Activity 4	Our Vision	26
Activity 5	Our Motto: "Welcome to Success"	29
Activity 6	Our Code of Conduct	36
Activity 7	Quieting Your Class	40
Activity 8	Procedural Charts	44
Activity 9	Assignment Board	54
Activity 10	Star of the Week	58
Activity 11	Words to Live By	63
Activity 12	Inspirational Quotes	69

Preparing to Interact with Parents

Activity 13	Popsicle Sticks	75
Activity 14	Parent Communication	77
Activity 15	Making Parents Feel Welcomed	84

Bonding with Students

Activity 16	The First Day of School	89
Activity 17	Greeting Students with TLC	92
Activity 18	Classy Compliment Tree	95
Activity 19	Fight-Free/Conflict-Free Bulletin Board	99
Activity 20	My Portfolio	101

Getting To Know Your Students

Activity 21	Gathering Information About Your Students	104
Activity 22	Why I Come To School	115
Activity 23	Personality Types	117
Activity 24	Learning Styles	124
Activity 25	Ways That I'm Smart	129
Activity 26	Who I Am	136

Ways of Preparing Students for Success

Activity 27   A Day In My Life 139
Activity 28   Responsible Choices 143
Activity 29   Traffic Light Book 145
Activity 30   Habits 149
Activity 31   Burying "I Can't" 153
Activity 32   Back Pack Book Club 156

Dream-Building Activities

Activity 33   Classroom Curriculum Goals 165
Activity 34   Personal Goals 168
Activity 35   Things We Dream of Doing 177
Activity 36   When I Graduate from Elementary School 180
Activity 37   Character Values 182
Activity 38   Let Me Tell You All About Me 185
Activity 39   MY DREAM 188
Activity 40   Let Me Tell You About My Dreams 191
Activity 41   How to Make My Dreams Come True 194
Activity 42   Things I Want To Learn 198
Activity 43   My Dream Collage 201
Activity 44   Mid-Year Student Assessment 203
Activity 45   Apprenticeships/Mentors 212
Activity 46   The Dream Tree 219
Activity 47   Dream Team Board 221
Activity 48   Guest Speaker Wall of Fame 224

Discovery Activities

Activity 49   Dream Portfolio 229
Activity 50   Dream Presentations 240
Activity 51   City Government 243
Activity 52   Models Alert 245
Activity 53   Aspiring Artists Club 249
Activity 54   Aspiring Writers Club 254
Activity 55   Radio/Television Broadcast Club 258
Activity 56   Guest Speakers 261
Activity 57   Dream Day Activities 267
Activity 58   Saying "Thank You" 269
Activity 59   Nice Things About You 272
Activity 60   Post-Assessment 274

Appendix
    Parkway School District's Character Values and Definitions
    Eagle Word List and Definitions
    Building Dreams Word List and Definitions

Bibliography

About the Authors

Mychal Wynn, co-founder of Rising Sun Publishing, has written several books and has presented workshops and keynote addresses throughout the United States, Canada, and the Caribbean. He has presented to such notable agencies, organizations, and school districts as: the California Conservation Corps, Kaufman Foundation, The Learning Exchange, Network of Cooperating Schools, MAD DADS, African-American Infusion Conference, National Conference for the Education of Black Children, National Conference on Preventing Crime in the Black Community, National Black Child Development Institute, National Alliance of Black School Educators, National Association of Black Social Workers, National Institutes of Health, Detroit Public Schools, Cleveland Public Schools, Dekalb County Schools (GA), Denver Public Schools, Indianapolis Public Schools, San Francisco Unified Schools, Los Angeles Unified Schools, Kansas City School District, North Chicago Public Schools, St. Louis Public Schools, Omaha Public Schools, Memphis City Schools, Griffin-Spalding Schools, the Tennessee Governor's Drug-Free Conference, The Ohio Commission on African-American Males, The National Council on Adoptable Children, The California Association of Compensatory Education, The National Coalition of Title I Parents, county schools throughout the states of South Carolina and Florida, South Carolina State University, Texas A & M University, the U.S. Virgin Islands Department of Education, and the Scarborough Board of Education in Toronto, Canada. Mychal's research activities have taken him into the African countries of Egypt and Ghana.

Mychal has engaged in over a decade of independent self-funded research into holistically structuring school, classroom, and home environments that optimize the opportunity for children to learn, to grow, and to succeed. Mychal has performed classroom demonstrations with students and trained thousands of teachers in meaningful and relevant strategies and techniques that has dramatically changed the lives of hundreds of thousands of America's children.

For his dedication, determination, and willingness to fight the battles to empower, enlighten, and inspire children, Mychal has received numerous community service awards including a special proclamation from the Governor of Indiana, the Mayor of Los Angeles, and Keys to the City of Bay City, Texas, Macon, Georgia, and Kansas City, Kansas.

Mychal, his wife, Nina, and their sons, Mychal-David and Jalani, live in Marietta, Georgia.

Dee Blassie is a teacher who is known for spending extra hours preparing for classes to make them interesting, enlivening and active learning experiences. Her dedication and knowledge base is reaffirmed when she takes extra time to see that each student learns, receives extra help and assistance when needed so that he/she may experience success. This time does not come from just the school day, it permeates into evenings and weekends. Parent phone calls, workshops for parents, and conferences are the status quo for Dee.

The benefits from Dee's work do not benefit only children. Teachers who come in contact with Dee cannot help but be influenced by her enthusiasm. She graciously shares her ideas and willingly presents to teacher groups. Dee is a twenty-four hour teacher and professional whose day does not end at 3:30, whose work week does not end on Friday afternoon, whose commitment to the ideals of her profession does not end with the semester or school year. She is a teacher who is available to students at all times to help, advise or just talk.

Dee's energy level, ideas, and acts of kindness have no limits. She serves on district and building-level committees as well as civic and community events/committees. She motivates not only her students but her colleagues as well. Her positive attitude and caring ways are contagious. Her care and concern for others is exemplified in her work. She is never too busy to listen to a colleague, offer a kind word or lend a helping hand. "Just tell me what I can do to help" are words often heard from Dee.

Dee is a teacher with character and integrity. She is honest, trustworthy, intelligent, compassionate, and understanding. She understands the problems of today's society with which children must deal and looks for ways to teach them coping and communication skills. She is a tireless worker and professional who adheres to the goals and objectives of public education.

— Virginia Altrogge
   Assistant Principal
   Carman Trails Elementary School
   Manchester, Missouri

Introduction

Dear Mychal,

Wow!! My dream came true in October and in March when I had the opportunity to learn about making dreams become a reality. I was so excited to do my first "Dream" presentation to 42 teachers from various schools throughout Parkway School District. They videotaped part of it. Would you like me to send you a copy of a "Dream Class?"

Educating a diverse population with diverse needs in a classroom of twenty-two or more children on a daily basis can be the most challenging yet frustrating job experienced. But with your ideas and my enthusiasm, we will set them all up for success.

As teachers, we provide a vital link to our most important natural resource, our youth. As educators, we are given the opportunity to daily support their basic needs and direct each student to identify the path to successful learning. We must provide our teachers with the proper training — the dream training — the Mychal Wynn training!!!

I'm sitting on the plane thinking of all the dreams that will become a reality. I'm so excited about your Dream concept. Count me in!!!

The day after I did a presentation on dreams, Ginny Altrogge, assistant principal, hugged me and said, "You motivated so many teachers. They want to take pictures of your classroom and want you to come back and speak again."

Enclosed is a list of themes that Ginny gave me after my presentation. I'll be back from Florida next Monday. Also, enclosed are some pictures of my "Dream Classroom." Can't wait to talk to you!

Fondly,

Dee Blassie

This letter is what prompted me to suggest to Dee Blassie that she and I develop this book together. In all of the training that I present before thousands of teachers throughout the U.S., Canada, and in the Caribbean, I am always looking toward providing teachers with practical tools to infuse into the fabric of their classrooms. My belief is that schools should be places of passion and purpose. That all children should come to school with dreams and aspirations and that what they learn, what they do, and what they experience in school should help them toward achieving their individual dreams and aspirations.

Some of the ideas and activities contained within this book were conceptualized by Dee and developed through her experiences over eighteen years of teaching. Other ideas and activities were conceptualized by me as a result of my writing, research, work with children, and beliefs. Still other ideas and activities were conceptualized by teachers, passed on to and expanded upon by other teachers, and eventually shared with or witnessed by either Dee or me. But no matter where the ideas were born and who expanded upon them, they represent energy within the universe which is available to anyone who wants to help children realize their potential.

I believe that the best teachers are constantly listening, watching, learning, implementing, and experimenting in the classroom to continually expand the effectiveness of what they do and how they do it. They then share their ideas and activities with anyone interested in teaching, mentoring, parenting, or in any way helping children. If I have one dollar and you have one dollar and we exchange dollars we are still left with but one dollar. However, if I have one idea and you have one idea and we exchange ideas we each have multiplied our capacity of ideas a hundredfold. This is the way it must be with teaching and parenting strategies. Through sharing we both can become twice as good at teaching and parenting as we were before.

We, at Rising Sun Publishing, are always looking for teachers, counselors, administrators, parents, and students, who not only are working toward their own dreams and aspirations but who are helping others toward theirs. I have met many teachers who are truly professional, caring, concerned, and genuinely loving individuals. I would like my own children to be in their classrooms. This describes Dee Blassie.

Harry K. Wong, in <u>The First Days of School</u>, notes three distinguishing characteristics of an effective teacher:

> An effective teacher has positive expectations for student success.
>
> An effective teacher is an extremely good classroom manager.
>
> An effective teacher knows how to design lessons for student mastery.

To add a fourth characteristic:

> An effective teacher listens to the dreams and aspirations of students and nurtures those students toward achieving richly rewarding and fulfilling lives.

Dee Blassie is the epitome of an effective teacher!

Mychal Wynn

An Effective Teacher

1. An effective teacher has positive expectations for student success.

2. An effective teacher is an extremely good classroom manager.

3. An effective teacher knows how to design lessons for student mastery.

4. An effective teacher listens to the dreams and aspirations of students and nurtures those students toward achieving richly rewarding and fulfilling lives.

© Rising Sun Publishing (800) 524-2813

How to Use This Book

The activities outlined in this book represent an holistically-integrated process: Positive language, classroom organization, procedural charts, multiple intelligences, learning styles, personality types, extracurricular and co-curricular activities are all integrated to structure a learning environment that nurtures the dreams and aspirations of children. This book is formatted in the sequence that we believe is most practical. The beginning activities should optimally be performed prior to the beginning of the school year. This allows the classroom teacher to set the tone during the first days of school for the entire school year. However, we realize that hundreds of teachers will be introduced to this material during the school year as a result of attending a staff development training, conference, purchasing the book, or by having someone who loves children pass the book on.

If you are introduced to this material during the school year don't say, "This is wonderful, I wish that I had this book at the beginning of the school year. I'm going to begin implementing these ideas next year!" Please, as a parent I don't want you to wait. I want my children to benefit from anything that you might learn during the school year that can help them to learn more effectively and experience a more rewarding year. Start today. Don't wait until next year. Simply say to your students, "I have some wonderful ideas about some things that we can do for the rest of the school year."

Read and reflect on the objectives for each activity and simply ask yourself, "How can my students benefit from this?" Keep a journal and note the types of behavioral changes, skills development, or other noticeable changes you witness in your students. You will be surprised at the end of the school year at the impact that some of the seemingly simple activities will have upon the lives, hopes, dreams, and aspirations of your students.

The activities are listed in a sequence that we believe is effective: Teacher Assessment, Preparing Your Classroom, Preparing to Interact with Parents, Bonding with Students, Getting To Know Your Students, Ways of Preparing Students for Success, Dream-Building Activities, and Discovery Activities.

We do not consider any of the activities too difficult for pre-kindergartners. However, children who have not developed the reading and writing skills required to complete an activity on their own can listen to activities being read to them. They can discuss or illustrate their dreams and aspirations, dictate, perform, or create dream story books. From K through 12, we believe in engaging children in a continual process of discovery, development, application, and internalizing. Discover the dream, develop the gifts, apply the knowledge, and internalize the spirit of the potential and possibilities. By raising our expectations, we help children to tap their limitless potential, even in pre-kindergarten.

In *Awakening Your Child's Natural Genius*, Thomas Armstrong notes:

> The whole-language approach to reading instruction should not be confused with the whole-word method, which focuses on memorization of sight words and the use of basal readers. Instead, whole language engages all aspects of a child's drive to communicate. Children spend their time, not hunched over worksheets, but actively involved in **reading and writing about things that passionately concern them**. They read real books—classic children's literature, adventure stories, poetry, how-to-do-it books, current events—not artificially contrived textbooks that lack controversy, conflict, and character development. Kids learn about language by using it every day in meaningful ways rather than by completing disconnected assignments bearing little relationship to real-life activities. In the kindergarten classrooms at PS 192 in New York City, for example, words are everywhere—on the windows, doors, floors, and chalkboards. Every child has his or her own special collection of favorite words, such as *helicopter* and *television*—words far too difficult to be used in a typical basal reader or phonics program but easily mastered by children when the words arise from their own **personal interests and concerns**. Kids dictate stories to the teacher and have them bound into little books that they can then read along with trade books in the classroom library.
>
> Instead of filling out worksheets and reading standard textbooks, children in a second-grade classroom at Crocker Farms Elementary School in Amherst, Massachusetts, study the life and work of Emily Dickinson. Students read her poetry, study biographies, visit her home (she was an Amherst resident) and then write about their experiences. "At any particular time," says their teacher, Susan Benedict, "it became impossible to decide if we were studying oral language, reading, writing. . . or social studies. . . At each step along the way there was time: time to talk, time to observe, time to question, time to investigate one topic, time to think, time to read, time to write."

Whole-language instruction helps students through the seamless communication process of reading, writing, spelling, handwriting, and grammar. Instead of dividing writing into separate skills, whole-language teachers emphasize the total experience of becoming literate. Students are motivated intrinsically through the process of becoming literate as they strive toward their dreams and aspirations.

The kindergartners at Welborn Elementary School in Kansas City, Kansas, can talk about their dreams. They can explain how "chicken" behavior can interfere with achieving their dreams. They have illustrated their dreams and have proudly posted them around the school. They have written books about their dreams, developed banners to celebrate their dreams, and asked engaging questions of guest speakers in an attempt to gather more information regarding their dreams. They have dressed as their dreams, talked about their dreams, and learned more about how to achieve their dreams and aspirations than many of America's high school students as a result of heightened expectations from a group of dedicated and talented teachers, the principal, and a support staff who are pursuing their own dreams. The principal and teaching staff at Welborn "expect" the students at Welborn to pursue their dreams.

The Animal School

Once upon a time, the animals decided they must do something heroic to meet the problems of a new world. So they organized a school. They adopted an activity curriculum consisting of running, climbing, swimming and flying. To make it easier to administer the curriculum, all the animals took all the subjects.

The duck was excellent in swimming; in fact, better than his instructor. But he made only passing grades in flying and was very poor in running. Since he was slow in running, he had to stay after school and also drop swimming to practice running. This was kept up until his webbed feet were badly worn and he was only average in swimming. But average was acceptable in school, so nobody worried about that except the duck.

The rabbit started at the top of the class in running, but had a nervous breakdown because of so much make-up work in swimming.

The squirrel was excellent in climbing until he developed frustration in the flying class where his teacher made him start from the ground up instead of from the treetop down. He also developed a charlie horse from overexertion and then got a "C" in climbing and a D in running.

The eagle was a problem child and was disciplined severely. In the climbing class, he beat all the others to the top of the tree, but insisted on using his own way to get there.

At the end of the year, an abnormal eel who could swim exceedingly well and also run, climb and fly a little, had the highest average and was valedictorian.

The prairie dogs stayed out of school and fought the tax levy because the administration would not add digging and burrowing to the curriculum. They apprenticed their children to a badger and later joined the groundhogs and gophers to start a successful private school.

Does this fable have a moral?

— George H. Reavis
Former Assistant Superintendent of the Cincinnati Public Schools

Why should we Build Dreams?

In staff development workshops, the question "Why should we build dreams?" is raised much more frequently than "How can we build dreams?" The "why" lies in the realities of the children whom you teach. If my children were in your classroom you wouldn't have to concern yourself with building their dreams. You should, but you wouldn't have to. My eight-year-old son already aspires to become a professional motorcycle racer (although that's a dream that I hope he changes). He aspires to become a professional artist, a dream that he will probably realize during his third grade year as he and I collaborate on a book together. He aspires to become a Black Belt in the Martial Arts, a dream that he will also realize during third grade (as this book goes to press he has just received his Brown Belt). My wife and I work many of the activities and all of the principles outlined in this book with our sons at home. We have identified their learning styles, personality types and highly-developed areas of intelligence. We provide them with exposure to a wide range of learning opportunities and applying what they've learned. My older son began demonstrating a love for drawing in the first grade. My wife and I realized that by amplifying his Visual/Spatial Intelligence through after school art [since our county schools do little to nurture the creative and performing arts] that his intrinsic motivation to learn would enhance his other intelligences [subsequently he tested for the talent and gifted program in second grade]. My wife and I are dedicated to ensuring that our children have every opportunity to discover and to pursue their dreams and aspirations. However, is such a child, who is developing higher-order thinking, placing the relevance of education in perspective to future career choices, developing the positive values and personal character to provide opportunities for himself, developing individual responsibilities, mannerisms, and a positive code of conduct, and being actively engaged in apprenticeship and actualization of his dreams and aspirations a typical student?

If you've been teaching for any period of time, you can tell which children have positive at-home support. They seem to catch on faster, apply what they've learned better, be more involved, and have more discipline and direction. They're usually the ones you enjoy teaching. But what about the others: those who lack self discipline, don't like school, don't like you as their teacher, won't do homework, think that school is dumb, don't see anything worth working toward in their futures, have a poor self image, little self respect, haven't learned to respect others and their property, and can be predicted to be among the millions of children who drop out or are pushed out of our schools? Will teaching them Reading, Writing, Arithmetic, Science, and Social Studies change their future? Do we care? What will we tolerate as our failure rate?

In workshops and seminars that I have presented, I have raised the question, "What are your major concerns about your school?"

Follow Your Dream

There was a young man who was the son of an itinerant horse trainer who would go from stable to stable, race track to race track, farm to farm and ranch to ranch training horses. As a result, the boy's high school career was continually interrupted. When he was a senior, he was asked to write a paper about what he wanted to be and do when he grew up.

That night he wrote a seven-page paper describing his goal of some day owning a horse ranch. He wrote about his dream in great detail and he even drew a diagram of a 200-acre ranch, showing the location of all the buildings, the stables, and the track. Then he drew a detailed floor plan for a 4,000-square-foot house that would sit on the 200-acre dream ranch.

He put a great deal of his heart into the project and the next day he handed it in to his teacher. Two days later he received his paper back. On the front page was a large red "F" with a note that read, "See me after." The boy with the dream went to see the teacher after class and asked, "Why did I receive an 'F' ?"

The teacher said, "This is an unrealistic dream for a young boy like you. You have no money. You come from an itinerant family. You have no resources. Owning a horse ranch requires a lot of money. You have to buy the land. You have to pay for the original breeding stock and later you'll have to pay large stud fees. There's no way you could ever do it." Then the teacher added, "If you will rewrite this paper with a more realistic goal, I will reconsider your grade."

The boy went home and thought about it long and hard. Finally, after sitting with it for a week, the boy turned in the same paper, making no changes at all. He stated, "You can keep the 'F' and I'll keep my dream."

The young man now lives in a 4,000-square-foot house in the middle of a 200-acre horse ranch. He has that school paper, "F" and all, framed above his fireplace.

— Jack Canfield, *Chicken Soup for the Soul*

Ten things that we *are* concerned with:

1) How do we reduce violence?

2) How do we structure safer classrooms?

3) How do we get students to accept responsibility?

4) How do we get students to take academic achievement seriously?

5) How do we motivate students?

6) How do we overcome dysfunctional families and the lack of positive reinforcement at home?

7) How do we overcome the lack of positive male role models?

8) How do we get students to stop putting each other down?

9) How do we get teachers to raise their expectations?

10) How do we get teachers to understand cultural differences between their students and families?

Notice that the question "How do we help children discover their dreams and aspirations?" is not on the list. Of the thousands of concerns expressed by teachers, parents, and administrators, this question hasn't even received honorable mention. The book, *Building Dreams: Helping Students Discover Their Potential,* raises ten areas that we should be concerned with if we are to transform our schools into places where our children want to go; that provide them with a supportive learning environment, and teach them things that are practical, tangible, and relevant to achieving their dreams and aspirations in life, and nurtures their development toward realizing their inherent gifts and natural potential. The book also outlines a number of components of what could be called a Dream-Building Classroom or Dream-Building School. The issues that all schools *should* concern themselves with and the major components are outlined on the following pages. These provide the basis for the activities outlined in this book.

The activities and classroom strategies contained in this book that are appropriate for elementary education incorporate many of the dream-building components that should exist in all schools and that have been uniquely applied in actual classroom settings by Dee Blassie and other extraordinary teachers.

Dee had been utilizing many of the teaching strategies and classroom organizational methods prior to being introduced to the Dream-Building process. Because Dee had been doing so many wonderful things with children in such areas as character values, conflict resolution, collaborative learning, and had created a non-threatening, risk-free learning environment, the dream-building components were an easy and natural fit. The academic goals were easily expanded into life goals. What students were learning was now made relevant to what they wanted to learn and where they wanted to go in life.

The activities outlined in this book are designed to holistically create a nurturing and supportive classroom environment. The holistic, integrated approach of these activities are designed to supplement the curriculum of the elementary-level teacher who wishes to foster cooperative learning, collaboration, support, encouragement, conflict resolution, character values, self esteem, positive self image, and create a non-threatening, risk-free learning environment where children want to learn and are motivated intrinsically to learn all that they can to achieve their individual dreams and aspirations.

The questions that should be raised regarding these activities are:

1) If I help my students to discover, develop, and pursue their dreams and aspirations will it keep fewer of them from failing?

   The answer is YES.

2) Will it help more students to make positive, healthy choices regarding their lives?

The answer is YES.

3) Will it increase the effectiveness of my classroom and the ability of my students to learn?

The answer is YES.

4) Will it require more work on my part?

The answer is YES.

If you currently have a well-run classroom, are teaching effectively, spending little time on discipline problems, have students actively working with each other, and are effectively managing your time, then you are going to be doing more work as you expand the scope of what you teach and engage students in dream-building activities. In doing so, you are going to tap your own wells of capacity as you lead children toward discovering their potential.

However, if this is not you, then you are probably going to achieve more with less work. You are going to spend more time on quality, fulfilling activities and less time on frustrating, energy-draining activities.

If you saw your concerns represented on the list of the ten things that we *are* concerned with, review the list on the following page of the ten things that we *should* be concerned with. Answering these questions is how we believe we can reduce the failure rate and make teaching and learning more rewarding, self-fulfilling, practical, relevant, and more fun!

I had a great feeling of relief when I began to understand that a youngster needs more than just subject matter. I know mathematics well, and I teach it well. I used to think that was all I needed to do. Now I teach children, not math. I accept the fact that I can only succeed partially with some of them. When I don't have to know all the answers, I seem to have more answers than when I tried to be the expert. The youngster who really made me understand this was Eddie. I asked him one day why he thought he was doing so much better than last year. He gave meaning to my whole new orientation. "It's because I like myself now when I'm with you," he said.

— A teacher quoted by Everett Shostrom in *Man, The Manipulator*

Ten things that we *should* be concerned with:

1) How do we engage children in an exploratory journey of their talents, abilities, innate interests, creative imaginations, personality types, and learning styles?

2) How do we help children understand the unique ways in which they learn and how to develop their special gifts and apply what they know?

3) How do we engage children in practical, meaningful, and relevant discussion, debate, and analysis of the real issues, challenges, and decisions that will confront them in their homes, communities, and the world around them?

4) How do we help children unlock their creative imaginations, tap their natural geniuses, express their creativity and individuality, and explore their innovativeness, in ways that may ignite a passion, dream, or aspiration?

5) How do we help children develop character values, habits, and choices consistent with achieving their dreams and aspirations?

6) How do we help children develop or acquire the skills, abilities, behavior, language, attitude, experiences, and knowledge that will allow them to achieve success in school that is consistent with achieving success in their lives?

7) How do we structure a nurturing, non-threatening and supportive learning environment that allows children to experience success at their individual developmental stages, competencies, and abilities?

8) How do we provide more opportunities for children to receive immediate feedback and intrinsic rewards through the practical application of what they're learning.

9) How do we provide children with a passion and purpose for going to school?

10) What do children want to learn?

© Rising Sun Publishing (800) 524-2813

Despite the amazing transformation of our children from the wide-eyed, energetic, inquisitive kindergartners to the apathetic, uninterested, uninvolved twelfth graders, few parents, teachers, or administrators express a concern with making school "more interesting." Although by law children are mandated to go to school, what and how much they learn is directly related to whether or not they "want" to go to school.

It is as though we have accepted the idea that after fourth grade school should no longer be fun, exciting, or interesting. That it is okay or natural that our children in large numbers no longer want to go. That our children should no longer work collaboratively and be supportive of each other. That we should no longer stimulate their senses and nurture their creative imaginations.

Our concerns are not focused on how we can correct what is wrong with our schools but on how we can correct what is wrong with our children. We want them to stop misbehaving. We want them to become more responsible. We want them to make more positive choices in effectively resolving their conflicts. We want them to take school more seriously. We want them to stop talking about and putting each other down. We want them to be motivated?

Motivated to do what? To be enthusiastic about walking through the corridors of a cell block? To be excited about the thousands of schools in America that are in disrepair and a perpetual state of decay? We want them to eagerly embrace a frequently intellectually bankrupted, irrelevant and abstract curriculum as they are told to sit still, be quiet, work hard, and never question why we are teaching what we teach and better yet never question why we are not teaching what they want to learn!

— Mychal Wynn, _Building Dreams: Helping Students Discover Their Potential_

Teacher Assessment

One of the most important components of a Dream-Building School or classroom is how well it is meeting the needs of the people in its school community. Sometimes an open and honest assessment is difficult to do because it implies, "If we're not doing what's being suggested, then we're doing it wrong!" However, in developing an environment that optimizes a teacher's ability to teach and a student's ability to learn, we are interested in continually evaluating where we are, what we're doing, and what fine tuning we may need to develop a *great* classroom and optimal learning experience.

> There was a little boy in November who didn't seem to want to come to school any more. His mother called me saying that he was faking a stomach ache and that he didn't want to come to school. Had he lost interest? Was he turned off to education? Was he having a problem with someone in school? Or, was it the unthinkable: Was I simply a bad teacher?
>
> I arranged for a meeting with James and his mother in our classroom and during the meeting I asked him, "James, was I a failure? What am I doing wrong? Am I not a good teacher?" But he said, "No Mrs. Blassie. You're cool. I just don't want to come to school."
>
> Then I asked James if there was something that he might like to do so that he could feel good about coming to school. He sat there and thought for a moment and said, "Yeah, I would like to be in charge of lining everyone up every day. No matter where we go, I want to be in charge." So I shared with the class the next day that we really wanted to help James to become successful. He would be in charge of organizing everyone. This would include lining everyone up daily each time we left class.
>
> How James had internalized and accepted ownership of this responsibility was revealed one day when a substitute teacher asked everyone to get in line. James politely got out of his seat and asked to speak with the substitute teacher outside in the corridor. Once outside, James told the substitute teacher, "Excuse me, Mrs. Blassie said that I could be in charge of lining everyone up because I didn't want to come to school. So, I think that I should continue my job!"

My informal survey of how James felt about school, my classroom, and about me as his teacher created an environment where a student could tell me what he needed to feel successful!

> The power is ours to determine our destination by the course of life that we follow, or to obscure it by the one that we fail to follow.
>
> — Bertha W. Richardson

I've come to a frightening conclusion that I am the decisive element in the classroom. It's my personal approach that creates the climate. It's my daily mood that makes the weather.

As a teacher, I possess a tremendous power to make a person's life miserable or joyous. I can be a tool of torture or an instrument of inspiration. I can humiliate or humor, hurt or heal.

In all situations, it is my response that decides whether a crisis will be escalated or de-escalated and a person humanized or de-humanized.

— Haim Ginott

Dream-Building School and Classroom Components

1) Pre-assessment/bonding
2) Cooperative learning environment
3) Student input/collaboration
4) Clearly-defined vision
5) Student-centered learning environment
6) Student/teacher ownership
7) Supportive, nurturing learning environment
8) Open discussion, debate, and sharing of ideas
9) Reverence toward the learning environment
10) Constantly expanding, changing curriculum
11) Verbal/visual affirmations of student dreams and aspirations
12) Validation/celebration of student-teacher diversity
13) Discovery of individual talents, gifts, and abilities
14) Celebration/recognition of multiple intelligences
15) Validation and acceptance of various learning styles
16) Validation, identification, and understanding of personality types
17) Positive, supportive, aesthetically stimulating school environment
18) Positive, supportive, collaborative school climate
19) Clearly-defined, visually-displayed school goals
20) Clearly-defined, visually-displayed curriculum goals
21) Data bank of information, mentors, opportunities, etc.
22) Special focus/interest groups
23) Schedule of guest speakers, field trips, learning opportunities
24) Strong alumni association and communication of alumnus achievements

Dream-Building School and Classroom Components (continued)

25) School-wide resource center
26) Teacher/student teams
27) Private partners
28) Utilization of technological resources
29) Positive student/staff relationships
30) Positive student/student relationships
31) Conscious focus on character development
32) Student dreams and aspirations infused into the curriculum
33) Special interest student and teacher planning time encouraging student choices
34) Active learning environment
35) Nurturing relationships
36) High self esteem
37) On-going evaluation
38) Focused and engaging curriculum with high achievement expectations
39) Strong library/media center
40) Opportunities for individual student success
41) Student portfolios
42) Apprenticeships
43) School-wide infusion of reading/cognitive activities
44) A self-governing professional teaching staff
45) Post-assessment evaluation

Have a dream!

Identify the steps toward achieving your **dream.**

Turn those steps into your **plan.**

Work on your plan throughout the school year.

Develop **positive habits.**

Make **healthy choices.**

Develop **character** traits consistent with achieving your dream.

Learn how to **cooperate** and **collaborate** with others.

Contribute to a positive classroom environment that helps everyone toward realizing their dreams.

Work hard and **don't make excuses!**

© Mychal Wynn/Rising Sun Publishing (800) 524-2813

Activity 1

Pre-Assessment

Objective

- To reaffirm some of the good things that we are doing in our classroom and assess what type of expanded classroom organization and structure we might consider.

Materials

- Teacher questionnaires for:
  - Classroom Environment
  - Inviting students/parents into your classroom
  - RESPECT [Responsibility, Encouragement, Support, Participation, Education, Collaboration, Trust]

Please complete the survey openly and honestly. There are no right or wrong answers. The questions were formulated to assess the types of things that we are already doing in our classrooms and what supplemental things we might consider.

I am not afraid to admit when I am wrong

Even though we know there is always room for improvement, we tend to shy away from criticism. Our egos tell us we are being attacked and quite naturally we want to strike back. In order to be whole, healthy beings, we need to know all there is to know about ourselves. Sometimes that information must come from others. This may mean admitting that we are not always right, and knowing it is okay to make a mistake. A mistake, an error, a poor choice, or bad decision does not equal "there is something wrong with me." It means you are on your way to being better. We do not make mistakes on the basis of race or color. We make them because we are human. When we acknowledge our errors and face up to our shortcomings, no one can use them against us.

— Iyanla Vanzant, *Acts of Faith*

Classroom Environment

Enter a "Y" for those things that you do. If you do not do these things consistently or if the question does not apply to you please leave the answer blank.

_____ 1. Are your signs and bulletin boards posted the first day of school?

_____ 2. Do you have inspirational signs posted?

_____ 3. Do you have an assignment calendar posted?

_____ 4. Do you have mobiles, clouds, etc., hanging from the ceiling with positive words and quotations?

_____ 5. Do you have character-building words posted?

_____ 6. Do you have inspirational words/phrases posted?

_____ 7. Do you have a Star or Special Student Corner?

_____ 8. Do you have procedural signs posted?

_____ 9. Do you have each student's name posted somewhere in the classroom?

_____ 10. Do you have a vision posted of what you want to achieve this school year?

_____ 11. Do you have pictures and images reflective of dreams, aspirations, and the diversity of your students posted?

_____ 12. Do you have each day's assignments and date posted before students enter class?

_____ 13. Do you greet your students with a smile, hug, or handshake with clear instructions for their first day of school?

_____ 14. Have you shared at least one great teaching technique with a colleague?

Inviting Students/Parents into Your Classroom

Enter a "Y" for those things that you do. If you do not do these things consistently or if the question does not apply to you please leave the answer blank.

_____ 1. Have you planned your first classroom activity which will initiate your first parental contact?

_____ 2. Are you planning to greet each student at the door every day that you are in class this school year?

_____ 3. Have you pre-planned your seating arrangements?

_____ 4. Are you planning to allow students' input into seating arrangements?

_____ 5. Do you have a back-to-school multiple intelligences activity planned?

_____ 6. Do you have a back-to-school learning styles activity planned?

_____ 7. Do you have a back-to-school personality type activity planned?

_____ 8. Do you refer to your classroom as *our* class rather than *my* class?

_____ 9. Do you have a planned activity for helping each student to discover their individual dreams and aspirations?

_____ 10. Do you have a schedule of activities that invite parents into the classroom?

_____ 11. Do you have a planned method of communicating to parents at least once a month what you've witnessed in their child?

_____ 12. Do you have a parent survey to assess parental resources that may be available to your classroom?

_____ 13. Do you have a system of special recognition for volunteers and guest speakers?

RESPECT
Responsibility, Encouragement, Support
Participation, Education, Collaboration, Trust

Enter a "Y" for those things that you do. If you do not do these things consistently or if the question does not apply to you please leave the answer blank.

_____ 1. Do you have an established method for demonstrating support for students who give wrong answers?

_____ 2. Do you have an established method for celebrating students who provide correct answers?

_____ 3. Do you have an established method for greeting guests into your classroom?

_____ 4. Do you have an established and consistently reinforced method of how students should enter class?

_____ 5. Do you have an established and consistently applied method of how students should exit class?

_____ 6. Do you have established methods for recognizing positive student behavior?

_____ 7. Do you have a bulletin board to affirm individual students', their dreams, goals, and aspirations?

_____ 8. Do you have established methods for recognizing collaborative student behavior?

_____ 9. Do you have established methods for recognizing fight-free or conflict-free behavior?

_____ 10. Do you have established methods for conflict mediation and resolution?

_____ 11. Do you have an established model of how students can formally compliment each other?

_____ 12. Do you have an established method for recognizing positive character values?

_____ 13. Do you have a planned activity for recognizing each student without regard to academic or skill level?

_____ 14. Do you have at least one curriculum activity which helps students understand and internalize responsible and respectful classroom behavior?

Total the number of Yes answers from all three and give yourself 1 point for each Yes answer. _____

What type of teacher are you?

The mediocre teacher tells
The good teacher explains
The superior teacher demonstrates
The great teacher inspires

— William Arthur Ward

35+   You are what William Arthur Ward describes as a *great* teacher.

30+   You are a *superior* teacher who recognizes the intangibles that contribute to positive classroom structure and a nurturing learning environment.

25+   You are doing a lot of good things and will probably give strong consideration to the ideas and activities that follow.

20+   You are doing some good things and should definitely give strong consideration to the ideas and activities that follow.

Less than 20   **We don't have a moment to lose!**

When fourth graders in a variety of classrooms (representing a range of teaching styles and socioeconomic backgrounds) were asked what their teachers most wanted them to do, they didn't say, "Ask thoughtful questions" or "Make responsible decisions" or "Help others." They said, "Be quiet, don't fool around, and get our work done on time."

. . . One way or another, millions of children learn to shut up and do what they're told. . . Children are rewarded for mindless obedience; the names of students who fail to obey are written on the blackboard for all to see; questions or objections are dismissed as irrelevant. All problems in the classroom are attributed to the students, and punishments imposed on them are said to result from their "choices."

— Alfie Kohn, *Punished by Rewards*

Activity 2

Invitational Learning Leads to Bonding

Objective

- To assess teacher behavior consistent with establishing a positive classroom environment.

Materials

- Teacher questionnaires for:
  - Invitational Comments
  - Invitational Behavior
  - Invitational Environment
  - Invitational Thoughts

William W. Purkey formulated a concept that has become known as "invitational learning." His concept helps us to focus on teacher language, behavior, environment, and thoughts that facilitate bonding with students. An inviting classroom is one in which students actively participate in classroom discussions; are willing to take risks, gain confidence and trust in the teacher; apply themselves more and increase self esteem. Such an environment can significantly reduce discipline problems.

We bond with students primarily through comments, behavior, and the physical environment that we structure, which are all, in large part, a direct reflection of what we think or believe about the children whom we are responsible for teaching. Although individual teacher behavior is a reflection of experiences and personality types, recognizing ways in which we could better bond with students can help alter our behavior and the language that we use to promote a healthy supportive learning environment.

When Peter J. Daniel was in the fourth grade, his teacher, Mrs. Phillips, constantly said, "Peter J. Daniel, you're no good, you're a bad apple and you're never going to amount to anything." Peter was totally illiterate until he was 26. A friend stayed up with him all night and read him a copy of _Think and Grow Rich_. Now he owns the street corners he used to fight on and just published his latest book: _Mrs. Phillips, You Were Wrong!_

In the first grade, Mr. Lohr said my purple tepee wasn't realistic enough, that purple was no color for a tent, that purple was a color for people who died, that my drawing wasn't good enough to hang with the others. I walked back to my seat counting the swish, swish, swishes of my baggy corduroy trousers. With a black crayon, nightfall came to my purple tent in the middle of an afternoon.

In second grade, Mr. Barta said, "Draw anything." He didn't care what. I left my paper blank and when he came around to my desk, my heart beat like a tom-tom while he touched my head with his big hand and in a soft voice said, "The snowfall. How clean and white and beautiful."

Inviting versus Uninviting Comments

Check either A or B in each pair of statements that *most* describes you.

____ A. "Good morning, how are you doing today?"

____ B. "Come in and take your seats."

____ A. "Thank you, that was a nice thing to do."

____ B. "So what do you want, a gold star?"

____ A. "That was an interesting observation."

____ B. "That's not what we were discussing."

____ A. "Let me help you find a better way."

____ B. "Will you stop doing that?"

____ A. "I'd like to know what you think."

____ B. "I don't care what you think."

____ A. "May I have your attention, please?"

____ B. "Okay, everybody quiet!"

____ A. "John, how can I help you to become more successful at turning your assignments in on time?"

____ B. "John, why don't you ever turn your assignments in on time?"

____ A. "What do you think I should do?"

____ B. "This is what I'm going to do whether you like it or not."

____ A. "Would you mind helping me collect papers?"

____ B. "Hey Ashley, collect the papers."

Inviting versus Uninviting Behavior

Check either A or B in each pair of statements that *most* describes you.

____ A. Eye contact and smiling.
____ B. Looking away or frowning.

____ A. Eye contact and listening.
____ B. Looking at your watch or yawning.

____ A. Looking at someone who walks into the room.
____ B. Ignoring someone who walks into the room.

____ A. Looking for an opportunity to help.
____ B. Looking for an opportunity to avoid helping.

____ A. Thumbs up or applause.
____ B. Scratching your head or making a face.

____ A. Nodding your head in approval.
____ B. Rolling your eyes.

____ A. Standing or offering someone a seat.
____ B. Sitting while they stand.

____ A. Shaking someone's hand.
____ B. Standing at a distance.

____ A. Calling someone by name.
____ B. Saying, "Hey, you!"

Inviting versus Uninviting Environment

Check either A or B in each pair of statements that *most* describes you or your classroom.

____ A.   Displaying personal photos, awards, certificates, etc.
____ B.   Desk and walls void of personal items.

____ A.   Places for others to sit.
____ B.   Place only for you to sit.

____ A.   Allowing easy access to you via the physical arrangement of furniture, desks, etc.
____ B.   Separating yourself from others by your arrangement of furniture, desks, etc.

____ A.   Plants, fresh smells, and fragrances in your classroom.
____ B.   Stale, bad smells, or odors in your classroom.

____ A.   Photos and student work on the walls.
____ B.   Bare walls or only commercial work.

____ A.   Photos, paintings, and other images that reflect student and teacher diversity.
____ B.   Photos, paintings, or other images that are largely void and unreflective of student/teacher diversity.

____ A.   Comfortable places for others to sit.
____ B.   Furniture that is old, rigid, or uninviting.

____ A.   Brightly-painted clean walls.
____ B.   Dull paint, cracking and peeling walls.

____ A.   Well-stocked supplies and resource materials.
____ B.   Little or no supplies and resource materials.

Inviting versus Uninviting Thoughts

Check either A or B in each pair of statements that *most* describes you.

____ A.   "I wonder how I can best help him to learn?"

____ B.   "He'd better listen and pay attention."

____ A.   "Let's see how many learning and processing styles I can determine."

____ B.   "These kids are so unprepared."

____ A.   "I can't understand why I haven't been able to reach her?"

____ B.   "She doesn't belong in a regular classroom."

____ A.   "He has such high energy I will have to find additional things for him to do."

____ B.   "That boy is so hyperactive."

____ A.   "She learns in special ways."

____ B.   "She's learning disabled."

____ A.   "I want to help all of my students to become successful."

____ B.   "I teach math."

____ A.   "How should I teach this year to reach this group of students?"

____ B.   "This is my class and I'm going to teach the way that I want to teach."

____ A.   "It's going to be interesting to see what their dreams and aspirations are."

____ B.   "These kids are lucky to still be in school."

Total the number of "A" answers from all three categories and give yourself 1 point for each "A" answer. _____

There were 36 possible ways to facilitate bonding with your students through your language, behavior, classroom environment, and thoughts.

Review your B answers and consider changing your comments, behavior toward others, classroom environment, and thoughts about your students. It is not enough to simply chalk it off as "That's my personality." Each of your students has his or her personality also. Bonding with your students and facilitating the ways in which they bond with each other will help them to learn and will help you to become a more effective teacher.

Do you have an inviting or uninviting classroom? Do your comments, behavior, ways you phrase questions, and physical environment invite students to risk trying and failing? If your students start the day out badly, is it made worse when they see you? If your students feel stupid before coming into your class, do they feel dumber when they leave? If your students feel small and unimportant before meeting you, the omnipotent educator, do they feel smaller and less important after meeting you?

— Mychal Wynn, *Building Dreams: Helping Students Discover Their Potential*

"I assume that pupils come to school with a distorted self-image. I take for granted their precarious self-respect. Therefore, in dealing with children I am cautious. I am aware that my comments touch on inner feelings. I am sensitive not to lessen self-esteem. I am careful not to diminish self-worth."

Unlike ships, human relations founder on pebbles, not reefs. A teacher can be most destructive or most instructive in dealing with everyday disciplinary problems. His instant response makes the difference between condemnation and consolation, rage and peace. Good discipline is a series of little victories in which a teacher, through small decencies, reaches a child's heart.

— Haim Ginott, *Teacher & Child*

I'm not learning-disabled, I'm eccentric

I began life as a learning-disabled child. I had a distortion of vision called dyslexia. So my first-grade teacher called me learning-disabled.

She wrote down her observations and passed them on to my second-grade teacher over the summer so she could develop an appropriate bias against me before I arrived. I entered the second grade able to see the answers to math problems but having no idea what the busy work was to reach them, and discovered that the busy work was more important than the answer. Now I was totally intimidated by the learning process, so I developed a stutter.

My third-grade teacher knew before I arrived that I couldn't speak, write, read or do mathematics, so she had no real optimism toward dealing with me.

I was about to die intellectually [as I entered the fifth grade], I entered the fifth grade and God placed me under the tutelage of the awesome Miss Hardy. This incredible woman, whose six-foot-frame towered above me, put her arms around me and said, "He's not learning-disabled, he's eccentric."

Now, people view the potential of an eccentric child far more optimistically than a plain old disabled one.

But she didn't leave it there. She said, "I've talked with your mother and she says when she reads something to you, you remember it almost photographically. You just don't do it well when you're asked to assemble all the words and pieces. And reading out loud appears to be a problem, so when I'm going to call on you to read in class, I'll let you know in advance so you can go home and memorize it the night before, then we'll fake it in front of the other kids. Also, Mom says when you look something over, you can talk about it with great understanding, but when she asks you to read it word for word and even write something about it, you appear to get hung up in the letters and stuff and lose the meaning. So, when the other kids are asked to read and write those worksheets I give them, you can go home and under less pressure on your own time do them and bring them back to me the next day."

I kept track of Miss Hardy over the years and learned a few years ago that she was terminally ill with cancer. Knowing how lonely she would be with her only special student over 1,000 miles away, I naively bought a plane ticket and traveled all that distance to stand in line (at least figuratively) behind several hundred other of her special students—people who had also kept track of her and had made a pilgrimage to renew their association and share their affection for her. The group was a very interesting mix of people—3 U.S. Senators, 12 state legislators and a number of chief executive officers of corporations and businesses.

The interesting thing, in comparing notes, is that three-fourth of us went into the fifth grade quite intimidated by the educational process, believing we were incapable, insignificant and at the mercy of fate or luck. We emerged from our contact with Miss Hardy believing we were capable, significant, influential people who had the capacity to make a difference in life if we would try.

— H. Stephen Glenn, *A 2nd Helping of Chicken Soup for the Soul*

Activity 3

Teacher Idea Board/Activity Book

Objectives

- To facilitate the sharing of ideas, classroom activities, and information between teachers and support staff.

- To provide a central location for gathering teacher activities, master letters, resources, etc.

Materials

- Construction paper.
- Centralized binder or filing cabinet.
- Push pins or thumb tacks.
- Paper.
- Pencils.

I would like to thank Sandy Pevey, media specialist at Fourth Ward Elementary School, in Griffin, Georgia, for creating the accompanying Teacher Activity form for the Fourth Ward Staff.

The Teacher Activity Book can provide a central, easily-accessible location for sharing ideas, activities, resources, and lesson plans. At most schools, each teacher (on the average) implements at least one powerful learning activity per year. The activity engages and excites, increases learning, and results in measurably increased skill development. However, most teachers develop a wealth of teaching strategies and activities that are rarely shared with colleagues. New teachers are hard pressed to "know what works."

Activities are often lost. The "Aha" experiences with children are rarely recorded. Thus, schools search each year for new ways of doing things. Think of how many teaching strategies, activities, and lesson plans one teaching staff could develop by simply capturing at least one positive activity from each teacher on the staff each year!

The Teacher Idea Board and Activity Book can provide an opportunity for teachers and support staff to share ideas quickly and effectively and save activities. Teachers pick up ideas and classroom activities throughout the school year as a result of attending staff development meetings, conferences, reading books and periodicals, etc. The Teacher Idea Board allows them an opportunity to share ideas and activities as they are recognized by their colleagues in doing so.

When we look at how children view a particular assignment, the relationship is even more impressive. One group of researchers tried to sort out the factors that helped third and fourth graders remember what they had been reading. They found that how *interested* the students were in the passage was **thirty times** more important than how "readable" the passage was.

. . .there may be some disagreement about why interested learners are likely to be effective learners, but the fact itself is had to dispute.

Alfie Kohn, *Punished by Rewards*

Procedure:

1) Identify a location for the idea board. An ideal location is in the central office or teachers' lounge.

2) Make pencils, note paper, and push pins readily available around the idea board.

3) Each idea can be written onto a sheet of note paper identifying the person sharing the idea together with a complete description of the idea.

4) Post the idea onto the idea board.

5) Consider creating categories on the idea board so that teachers can gather ideas by category, such as:
   - Self esteem
   - Content areas
   - Dream-building activities
   - Conflict resolution
   - Cooperative learning
   - Classroom organization
   - Bonding
   - School-wide activities
   - Skills development
   - Community service

6) Teachers can also be encouraged to share the positive results of various ideas that they picked up from the idea board.

7) Create a binder or file cabinet location with tabs that allow activities to be separated into such categories as those mentioned above.

8) Use the form on the following page for recording activities.

9) Post the activities and develop a system for reward or recognition for teachers who contribute activities such as:

   A. Most innovative

   B. Most activities contributed

10) Publish an activities book each year and use the activities to drive teacher training and staff development.

Teacher Activity Form

Date: _____

Author(s): _____

_____

Contributing Teacher(s): _____

_____

Academic Subject: _____

Specific Topic: _____

Suggested Grade Level(s): _____

Objectives: _____

_____

Materials: _____

Overview of Activity (attach a detailed plan):

_____

_____

_____

Observations: _____

_____

_____

_____

Classroom Environment

How a teacher structures the classroom is often a function of the unique personality type of the teacher. It would be fine if this was the teacher's home and he/she didn't need to be concerned about how much he or she should go out of the way to make others feel comfortable in that home. "After all, my home is *my* home. I arrange the pictures, the furniture, the flowers, etc., the way that I want them. I use the color paint that I want and that is pleasing to my personality. And, oh do I get angry when someone takes something from where I placed it and puts it somewhere else!"

You may have heard colleagues comment, "This is *my* classroom and I'm going to organize it the way that works best for me!" Well honey, just consider that you are about to have 20 to 30 little people coming into your home. They're going to come to you out of 20 to 30 different households, cultures, environments, and experiences. They may not value what you value; they may not see life the way you see it; they may not be clean; they may not be well fed; they may have never been taught how to conduct themselves in public; they may have developed many bad habits; they may have negative attitudes toward teachers or anyone in authority; they may suffer from low self image and poor self esteem; they may lack personal responsibility; they may lack effective conflict resolution skills; and, they may have experienced teachers in the past who made them feel unimportant, small, ugly, stupid, unclean, and unwanted.

If we want to prepare them, and ourselves, to become successful this school year, then we want them to feel welcomed: take ownership of *our* classroom, feel that this is a place where they can try and fail without fear of put down or ridicule; a place where they will encourage each other and work together perhaps in ways that they have never worked together with people in their own households.

We can only achieve this by relinquishing ownership of our classroom and by viewing each classroom as a village within a larger school community. To optimize our success we need to draw upon the skills, talents, special abilities, and gifts of each person in the village. This can only be achieved if each of the people in the village feels valued and important. Each student, parent, teacher, and support staff must feel they have something valuable to contribute to the village and that the success of our village is dependent upon each of us.

Have you ever walked through a hallway and seen trash on the floor? Countless other students and teachers may have walked past that same trash but no one stopped to pick it up. No one took ownership. It was not theirs.

Have you ever known a colleague who presented effective lessons and who effectively bonded with their students, but they have never shared their strategies or techniques with other teachers? They did *their* things in *their* classrooms but they didn't take ownership of the larger school community. They had *their* classrooms, but it was not *their* school.

We must model for our students the values that will sustain society. Collaboration, cooperation, responsibility, and respect are integral components of the evolution of civilization. Students must feel a part of and become contributing members to our classroom village and school community. Sure, a great teacher can do it alone; however, it is so much more valuable to the growth and development of students when we do it together!

For the most successful Japanese companies, there is only one system: *Kaizen*—continuous improvement. Not a day goes by without meaningful improvement in companies that use Kaizen. They have to use it in order to stay competitive and remain valued suppliers of goods and services. . . the day-in-day-out process of Kaizen—of continuous improvement—requires successful implementation of a series of ideas—large, small, and also those in between. And that involves every person in the company—at every level—in thinking about the process of work and suggesting and implementing improvements.

— Martin Edelston, *I Power*

Activity 4

Our Vision

Objectives

- To establish a vision that explains how we see our classroom and how we intend to collaborate and cooperate with each other.

- To help students focus on why we are working together as a team.

Materials

- Blow up a vision statement or create one that you feel grade-appropriate for your classroom.

"When you walk into our classroom everyone should feel successful. For that to happen, we all need to share expectations and exhibit behaviors that will help us to become a successful Classroom."

The vision statement on the following page was taken from the book, *Building Dreams: Helping Students Discover Their Potential*. It reinforces our theme of "Welcome to Success." It also helps each student to understand what we must believe about each other to help each other achieve our individual dreams and aspirations.

Blow the vision statement up into poster size and have each student sign it or place a hand print or thumb print on it. Have a beginning of the year classroom discussion about what it means to have a vision; to have a dream that will guide them toward a destination in life. Refer to the vision continually throughout the school year as you relate their behaviors, attitudes, willingness to work together, etc., as being in support or in conflict with your classroom vision.

Bring your vision to the attention of visitors to your classroom and call upon different students to explain your vision and how they are working to achieve the vision.

Marva Collins, founder of Westside Preparatory School in Chicago, Illinois, articulates such a vision, ". . .[We have] a total program that teaches all children that they are unique, special, and that they are too bright to ever be less than all that they can be. The 'I will not let you fail' statement is one that they seldom hear elsewhere.

As I listened today to three- and four-year-olds reading about Daedalus and Icarus, one four-year-old declared: 'Mrs. Collins, if we do not learn and work hard, we will take an Icarian Flight to nowhere.' I somehow wished that the whole world could see and understand that all children are born achievers and all they need is someone to help them become all that they have the potential to become."

— Marva Collins, *Ordinary Children, Extraordinary Teachers*

Our Vision

Our vision is that every student, parent, teacher, staff member, administrative support person, and all who enter this school will enter into a field of dreams:

A PLACE WHERE DREAMING IS ENCOURAGED, NOT DISCOURAGED.

WHERE DREAMING IS SUPPORTED, NOT CONDEMNED.

A PLACE WHERE IDEAS ARE DEVELOPED AND OPPORTUNITIES ARE DISCOVERED.

A PLACE WHERE IT'S BETTER TO TRY AND FAIL THAN TO HAVE NEVER TRIED.

A PLACE OF ACHIEVERS, NOT A PLACE OF QUITTERS.

Everyone who enters into our field of dreams is recognized as having the capacity for learning. Every student is recognized as gifted. Part of our responsibility is to help them discover their giftedness.

Every person entering our field of dreams is deserving of the highest level of respect, support, and encouragement.

Our school environment, curriculum, classroom organization, student government, code of conduct, teacher-staff-administrative attitudes, and student behaviors must all be in support of our vision.

We are not in competition between ourselves, but on a never-ending journey to discover the best within ourselves. Each of us can make a difference.

This is our Vision. This is why we are here.

© Mychal Wynn/Rising Sun Publishing (800) 524-2813

Activity 5

Our Motto: "Welcome to Success"

Objective

- Create a classroom slogan that:
    - Communicates expectations
    - Nurtures self esteem
    - Welcomes students
    - Makes students feel at home
    - Provides a visual image of important concepts to be reinforced throughout the school year

Materials

- Construction paper.
- Scissors (other materials depending upon the scope of your individual creativity).

"Good morning, my name is Mrs. Blassie and I want to prepare you to become successful this year. I want you to help me to help you become successful. I want you to help me to become a more successful teacher."

"Do you think that by yelling and screaming at you I will help you to become successful? Or, would talking to you calmly and helping you to better understand and learn things help you to become successful?"

"Do you think that laughing at people and putting them down will help them to become successful? Or, would giving them a thumbs up when they try, giving them applause when they get a right answer, and encouraging and supporting them help them to become successful?"

"Well, we're going to do everything we can this year to help each other to become successful. Beneath our 'Welcome To Success' sign is our 'Welcome To Success Suggestion Mailbox.' Any time you think of an idea, something that we can do in our classroom or a better way to support each other, write your idea down on an idea sheet and place it into our 'Welcome To Success Suggestion Mailbox' and lift the mailbox flag so that we know that we have new suggestions. To be successful requires hard work, a positive attitude, strong character, and a willingness to work together and share ideas. But isn't it worth putting in a little hard work and having a positive attitude to be successful?"

"Welcome to Success," this is my favorite sign. It's a motto that I constantly refer to. I am constantly asking students, throughout the school year, "How can I help you to become successful?"

Creative imagination forms the mold through which the Creative Process of Life works to produce the manifest Universe. The chair upon which you sit was first an *idea* in someone's mind. This idea was translated into a visual image in that person's mind. Out of that image came the physical expression of the idea. The great Albert Einstein said, "Imagination is more important than knowledge."

— Jack Addington

Procedure:

1) Using construction paper, cut out the letters for your motto.

2) Post in an area which students frequently face.

3) Create a box or mailbox where students can place ideas. Call it your "Success Suggestion Box" or "Idea Box," or "How We can help each other Succeed Box."

4) Have all of the students say the "Welcome to Success" chant each day as class begins.

In addition to this first day of school dialogue, I consciously phrase questions throughout the school year to reaffirm to my students that I am committed to helping them to become successful. It's important to a student to believe that you care about them and that you're sincere. This confidence helps your students to establish trust in you and to develop a willingness to work together in the classroom.

Sample dialogue:

"How can I help you to become successful?"

"Can you help me to become a more successful teacher?"

"Will you help me to help your child become successful?"

"How can I help you to become more successful at turning in your assignments?"

"Does laughing at people help them to become successful?"

"Does encouraging and supporting people help them to become successful?"

"Is there anything else we can do to so that each of us has the most successful year possible?"

Our classroom chant on the following page supports our motto.

Are your students helping each other to become successful?

I was the worst student in my whole fifth-grade class. After we'd taken a test someone would invariably say, "I know what Carson got!" "Yeah! A big zero!" another would shoot back. "Hey, dummy, think you'll get one right this time?" "Carson got one right last time. You know why? He was trying to put down the wrong answer."

— Ben Carson, <u>Gifted Hands</u>

Ben Carson, the worst student in his fifth grade class would go on to receive an academic scholarship to Yale University, graduate from the Michigan Medical school, and at the age of 33 become the director of pediatric neurosurgery at John's Hopkins Hospital in Baltimore, Maryland, and become the first surgeon to successfully separate Siamese twins join at the back of the head!

Welcome to Success

Welcome to Success.

A place where we do our best.

We respect, encourage, and support each other.

We never laugh at, put down, or discourage another.

We may be children, but we have great dreams.

Working together we can achieve anything.

Welcome to Success.

A place where we do our best.

© Rising Sun Publishing (800) 524-2813

The WELCOME TO SUCCESS sign awaits you in Mrs. Blassie's classroom above the aboard "The Spotlight is on You," and "Fight-Free" board.

How one teacher helped a student become successful

Bert, age ten, specialized in interruptions. He lent his tongue to every conversation, uninvited. He shared his views on every subject, unasked. He meddled in foreign affairs and contributed irrelevancies to every interchange. His public proclamations taxed the patience of his teacher and his classmates. Bert ignored all rebukes and reprimands. He even interrupted the criticism about his interruptions. In desperation, the teacher wrote him the following note:

Dear Bert,

I am writing to enlist your cooperation. Please limit yourself to two verbal comments during each period. If you have something more to contribute, say it in writing. Use the enclosed notes and envelopes to mail me your comments. I am looking forward to your private correspondence.

Sincerely,

Your Teacher

Bert felt flattered to receive a letter from the teacher addressed to him. He read and reread it and made an effort to comply with the request.

— Haim Ginott, *Teacher & Child*

TO ALL STUDENTS:

If you have an idea that would help in running our class, I would like to know about it. Please use the form below, and return it to me whenever you have an idea.

Sincerely,

Name: _____ Date: _____

I have an idea!

_____

_____

_____

Please explain how this idea will help our class:

_____

_____

_____

_____

_____

_____

_____

Wynn/Blassie • © 1995 Rising Sun Publishing • (800) 524-2813
Building Dreams: Elementary School Edition Teacher's Guide

Your classroom motto can also be in the form of a classroom pledge such as the one created by Sharon Moazzen, a teacher at Graceland Elementary School in Kansas City, Missouri, that is recited by her students each morning.

Our Class Pledge

I like who I am this morning.

I like who I am this morning.

I like who I am this morning.

Therefore, I am going to be good to me today.

I pledge to learn more about my community, my friends, and the world around us.

I pledge to accept the knowledge I gain as:

POWER (shout!)

Power, as the opportunity to be the best I can be.

Why? Because I am special and I like who I am this morning.

"How are we feeling this morning?"

EXCELLENT (shout!)

Activity 6

Our Code of Conduct

Objectives

- To establish a classroom model for student behavior.

- To clearly communicate expectations to facilitate effective classroom management.

- To provide visual aides for dealing with student behavior.

Materials

- Large poster board or pre-printed posters.

  Note: Regular 8 1/2 x 11 sheets can be printed professionally on school computers and blown up into poster size at local print shops and photocopy centers.

A classroom or school-wide code of conduct should be age-appropriate and provide a visual reference to those issues, behaviors, and student conduct that typically reveal themselves in the classroom and throughout the school. Such a chart could be called a "Code of Conduct," "Commitment to Our School," "Citizenship Code," etc.

The purpose of the chart is to provide a visual affirmation of appropriate behaviors that you can refer to continually throughout the school year whenever students demonstrate behavior inconsistent with your "setting them up for success."

The following activity will help you develop your visual affirmation, student verbal declaration, and student written affirmation of the appropriate behaviors in your classroom.

Procedure:

1) Develop a Code of Conduct that is age-appropriate.

2) Label the code of conduct chart [i.e., Code of Conduct, Citizenship Code, Commitment to Ourselves, etc.].

3) Blow up to poster size.

4) Discuss with your students and have a ceremony in which all of your students make a written declaration by signing, placing a hand print, or thumb print, etc., onto the code of conduct.

5) Have your students provide a verbal affirmation by reciting the code of conduct.

6) Post the chart in the classroom and refer to it whenever the behaviors outlined on your code of conduct reveal themselves.

Sample dialogue:

"Nicole, by hitting Mark, what code of conduct did you violate?"

"Ashley, by leaving your assignment at home what code of conduct did you violate?"

"Mychal-David, by jumping in front of the line, what code of conduct did you violate?"

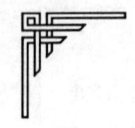

Our Commitment to Our School

1. We will come on time, be prepared, and be ready to learn.

2. We will be responsible for our actions and respectful of others.

3. We will be honest.

4. We will take pride in using good manners.

5. We will be respectful of authority and school rules.

6. We will demonstrate compassion, integrity, intelligence and determination.

7. We will cooperate with each other and compete only against ourselves.

8. We will strive for excellence in what we do. Anything worth doing is worth doing well.

9. We will work toward our dreams and be encouraging of the dreams of others.

10. We will not make excuses.

© Mychal Wynn/Rising Sun Publishing (800) 524-2813

Wynn/Blassie • © 1995 Rising Sun Publishing • (800) 524-2813
Building Dreams: Elementary School Edition Teacher's Guide

The following code of conduct was developed by Buena Vista Elementary School in Greer, South Carolina, and was named the "Buena Vista Citizenship Code."

Buena Vista Citizenship Code

1. We will come on time, be prepared, and ready to work.

2. We will begin and end each day with a positive attitude.

3. We will begin each day with a friendly greeting and a smile.

4. We will strive to be honest and respectful.

5. We will strive for excellence in all that we do. Anything worth doing is worth doing well.

6. We will take pride in using good manners.

7. We will show respect for ourselves and for the rights and property of others.

8. We will say positive and encouraging things to each other.

9. We will not make excuses.

10. We are responsible for ourselves and will work together.

Activity 7

Quieting Your Class

Objectives

- To establish a procedure for quieting your class and gaining your students' attention.
- To clearly communicate your expectations.

Materials

- Procedural chart.

Help your class to help you prepare them to become successful. Develop the procedures for quieting them and gaining their attention in such places as the classroom, school corridors, playground, auditorium, field trips, etc. Keep in mind that your ability to quickly gain their attention helps to keep them safe, teaches them how to be respectful of adult authority, and encourages them to be responsible and self directed.

In many schools teachers fail to do this because they have lowered their expectations of students until they don't believe that their students are capable of behaving in a self directed and respectful way. If we do not teach this type of behavior in school, how can we possibly prepare them to become successful?

"Class, to best help me prepare you to become successful I am going to need your cooperation when it is time to be quiet and respectfully listen to the teacher or another speaker."

Procedure:

1) Decide upon your procedure. Remember that your procedure communicates your expectations. If you expect your students to behave like a bunch of wild, disrespectful, uncontrollable children, then you probably will yell and scream at them a lot. However, if you expect your students to seriously work together as they continue toward their dreams and aspirations, then you will decide on an appropriate procedure that communicates the highest expectations.

2) Explain the procedure to your students.

"Class, whenever I do this, I want everyone to immediately follow this procedure. If one of your classmates doesn't know what to do, politely and quietly tell him or her that it's quiet time and I would like for you to be responsible and continue to follow the procedure."

3) Ask individual students to repeat the procedure to you.

4) Have the entire class repeat the procedure.

5) Continue to rehearse the procedure until you are confident that all of your students understand the procedure.

When the teacher says:

"May I have your attention:"

1. Stop moving.

2. Stop talking.

3. Look at the teacher.

4. Listen to the teacher.

5. Follow instructions.

Building Dreams: Elementary School Edition © 1995 Rising Sun Publishing (800) 524-2813

When the teacher:

"Raises a Hand"

1. Raise your right hand.
2. Stop talking.
3. Look at the teacher.
4. Listen to the teacher.
5. Follow instructions.

Building Dreams: Elementary School Edition © 1995 Rising Sun Publishing (800) 524-2813

Activity 8

Procedural Charts

Objectives

- To establish classroom procedures for dealing with important issues.

- To clearly communicate expectations to facilitate effective classroom management.

- To provide visual aides for facilitating classroom management.

- To provide a consistent, clearly-communicated, fair way of dealing with issues and conflicts.

Materials

- Large poster boards or pre-printed posters.

   Note: Regular 8 1/2 x 11 sheets can be printed professionally on school computers and blown up into poster size at local print shops and photocopy centers.

"To have an effective learning environment for the time we will be together this year, we need to establish procedures that we all understand. We will read and discuss, on a daily basis for two weeks, what is expected of you in different situations. We will continue to review the procedures as long as necessary for you to be comfortable using them."

"Class, you'll notice that around the room I have posted different procedural charts. Who can tell me what a procedure is?"

"Let's go over each of the classroom procedural charts to make sure that everyone understands how we are going to be working together this year."

Procedure:

A procedural chart can be developed for any area where you have dealt with issues in the past (e.g., behavior, work/study habits, individual responsibility, diversity, etc.). We cannot underscore how valuable procedures can be to helping students remain focused on expected and acceptable classroom behavior.

Procedural charts help students develop regular routines and ways of dealing with issues, behavior, etc. in class. It encourages them to accept ownership, be responsible, and self directed in their behavior.

Procedural charts don't have to be big. Depending upon what is being communicated, they can be as small as a single word, sentence, or phrase.

After the procedures are discussed and agreement is solicited from students, adjustments should be made if necessary.

"Can we live with this? Remember this is *our* classroom! I believe that these procedures will help us to have a smooth-running classroom this year so that we can help each other become successful."

Several typical procedural charts are on the pages that follow. They can be blown up and used as-is, or you may adapt them to the appropriate grade level and student population.

Support Each Other

When someone attempts to answer a question and they give the wrong answer:

Give them a thumbs up for trying!

When someone gives the correct answer to a question:

Applaud them for their success!

Building Dreams: Elementary School Edition © 1995 Rising Sun Publishing (800) 524-2813

When We Enter Class

1. Say good morning to the teacher.

2. Put away outdoor clothes.

3. Stop using outdoor voices.

4. Take out books and supplies.

5. Begin working.

Building Dreams: Elementary School Edition © 1995 Rising Sun Publishing (800) 524-2813

When Class Ends

1. Put things away and clean up work area.

2. Get outdoor clothes if necessary.

3. Line up responsibly behind whomever is in charge of the line.

4. Wait for the teacher's instructions.

Building Dreams: Elementary School Edition © 1995 Rising Sun Publishing (800) 524-2813

When We Have A Conflict

1. We attempt to be responsible and resolve it ourselves in a peaceful and respectful manner.

2. If we are unable to resolve it ourselves, we ask the teacher for a conflict mediation meeting.

Building Dreams: Elementary School Edition © 1995 Rising Sun Publishing (800) 524-2813

In Our Classroom

When we have a visitor:

1. Our classroom ambassador greets them.

2. Our class recites our welcome.

When we have a substitute teacher:

1. Our classroom ambassador greets them.

2. The teacher's assistant explains our Classroom Procedures.

3. We begin our assignments.

Building Dreams: Elementary School Edition © 1995 Rising Sun Publishing (800) 524-2813

Be Responsible

1. Bring your assignment folder to school each day.

2. Check the board for daily assignments.

3. Check the assignment calendar for missed assignments.

4. When absent from school, call a classmate.

Building Dreams: Elementary School Edition © 1995 Rising Sun Publishing (800) 524-2813

In Our Classroom

1. We are honest.

2. We are respectful.

3. We are supportive.

4. We are encouraging.

5. We are responsible.

Building Dreams: Elementary School Edition © 1995 Rising Sun Publishing (800) 524-2813

How We Answer Questions

1. Raise hand.

2. Wait until called upon.

3. Answer in a complete sentence.

Building Dreams: Elementary School Edition © 1995 Rising Sun Publishing (800) 524-2813

Activity 9

Assignment Board

Objectives

- To establish a procedure for communicating assignments.
- To help students track their own work, thereby building responsibility.
- To prepare students for becoming self directed and for assuming responsibilities in the workplace.
- To reduce teacher interruptions. (Whenever students are absent they can go to the board for their assignments.)
- To prepare students for maintaining their own individual assignment books.
- To encourage individual responsibility.
- To provide a visual aide for visual learners.

Materials

- Large laminated or washable monthly calendar.

The assignment board is a monthly calendar that shows all monthly assignments.

"Good morning. To help you to become successful, I'll post your daily assignments on the assignment board in the same place."

"You can come in to class every day and get your day started in a successful way. If you're absent, all your papers will be located below the calendar in the appropriate folders labeled: Math, Science, Social Studies, and so forth. If you have any questions please feel free to ask me or your partner."

Procedure:

1) Model how to note the assignments on the assignment calendar for the first two weeks.

2) The student Star of the Week, Classroom Ambassador or other designated student is responsible for noting the assignments thereafter.

3) During the first nine weeks, student assignment sheets have to be signed daily by parents.

4) Contact parents after the first nine weeks, asking them if they feel that they need the assignment sheets to continue.

5) A laminated assignment calendar can be re-used throughout the school year. Allow your students to help clean the assignment calendar and renumber the days.

6) Keep assignment folders below the assignment calendar so that students don't have to ask for their assignments or copies of the instructions.

We believe it is considerably more effective, both in the short and long range, to help all students—"at-risk" or not—to learn how best to help themselves become successful learners.

Not only do all children have the potential for creative accomplishment, but all children should have goals that will challenge them and a vision that will lead them to be the best they can be.

— Dunn, R., Dunn, K., and Treffinger, D. _Bringing out the Giftedness in your Child_

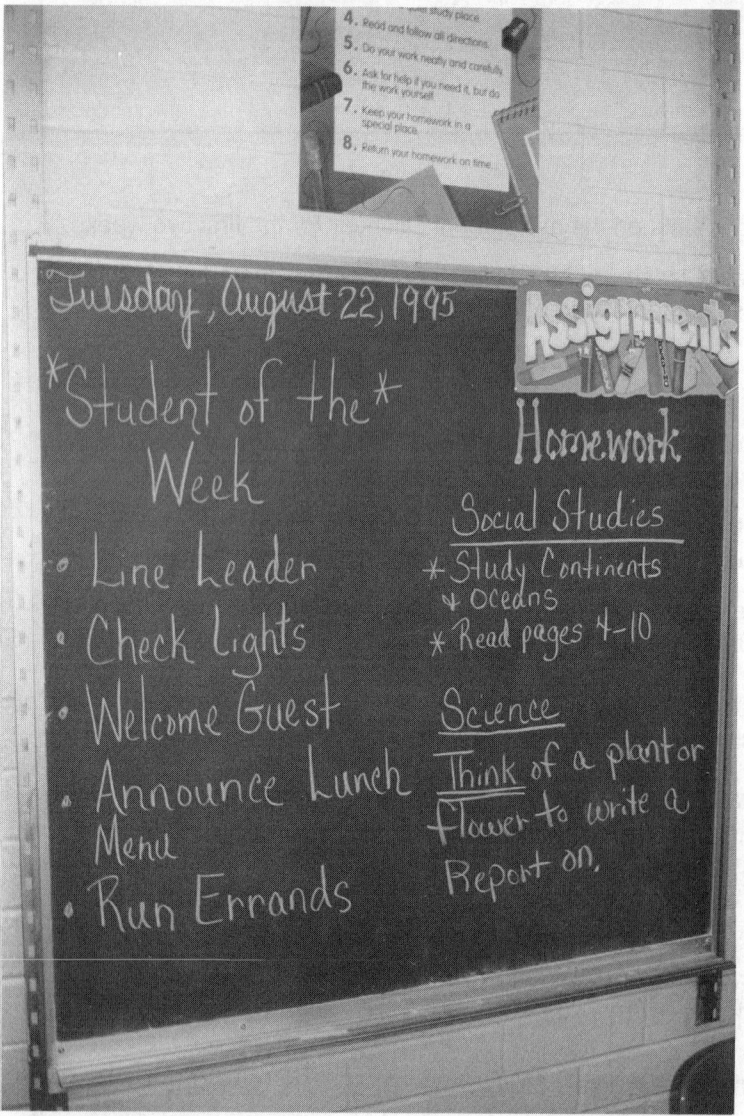

[Above] A high school student in Mrs. Blassie's Cadet Teacher program stands in front of the Assignment Calendar easily accessible to students.

[Left] In another classroom the daily assignments are clearly posted on the board together with the Student of the Week responsibilities.

Wynn/Blassie • © 1995 Rising Sun Publishing • (800) 524-2813
Building Dreams: Elementary School Edition Teacher's Guide

ASSIGNMENTS FOR: _____

Subject	Mon	Tue	Wed	Thur	Fri	Sat

©Rising Sun Publishing • (800) 524-2813

Activity 10

Star of the Week

Objectives

- To provide each student with an opportunity for individual attention and recognition.
- To enhance language skills.
- To enhance self esteem.
- To encourage appreciation of diversity.
- To help students accept responsibility.
- To provide a fun parent-student activity.

Materials

- Plastic or cloth shopping bag.
- School year calendar for parents to select a week.
- Reminder forms for parents.
- Parent letters.
- Construction paper.
- Spot light.

A fun way to begin this activity is to model yourself as the Star of the Week.

"I'd like you to help me celebrate my dream of being your teacher. As you can see from the photos of my early childhood to the present, I enjoy helping others."

Procedure:

1) Go through all of your pictures explaining how your dreams became a reality. Bring your awards, certificates, momentos, etc., to share.

2) At the end of the week, bring a treat to share with the class.

3) If you have a child, spouse, mom, dad, etc., ask them to visit during your special week to read a story or do an activity.

"I invited my husband, Tom; daughter, Angela; her husband, Nathan; and my granddaughter, Haylye. The children loved it! Of course my husband brought in treats for the students."

Expanded Activity:

Mary Hujik, a second grade teacher at Mt. Bethel Elementary School in Marietta, Georgia, has a bulletin board decorated with a square for every student in her class. Each student has a star with his/her name on it that he/she can place into any square. That square becomes his/her special square for the entire school year. Each week students can bring something special to post into their individual squares. E.g., photos, certificates, school work, etc.

Each student in the class will have an opportunity to receive special recognition, accept individual responsibilities, and receive compliments from other students. Each student has an opportunity to share things about himself/herself and has an opportunity to work together with their parent(s) on a fun activity.

Purpose:

1) To provide each student with an opportunity for individual attention and recognition.

2) To provide each student with a full week of individual classroom responsibilities.

3) To engage students in a practice exercise of complimenting, supporting, and appreciating each other.

4) To provide individual students with an opportunity to share information about themselves, their families, and their cultures.

5) To provide students with a fun activity to be performed with their parent(s).

Procedure:

1) "During Open House I post a calendar and allow parents to select a week that they would like their child to be the Star of the Week."

2) "I make a poster and place 9 index cards—one for each month starting with September through June."

Please sign your child up for being the Star of the Week. You might want to have your child's special week on his/her birthday.

3) Present parents with a letter after they have signed up at Open House for their special week (see next page).

4) Send a reminder home a week before and follow-up with a reminder the Friday before (see letters).

5) Decorate the Star of the Week bulletin board with lights, a border, and a sign: STAR OF THE WEEK.

6) Use yourself as the first Star of the Week to model for your classroom and their parents.

7) Give each student the Star of the Week basket on the Friday before to bring their things to school for the following week.

8) The Star of the Week must write something about himself/herself, the things that he/she likes to do, things that he/she would like to do in the future, and what his/her dreams and aspirations are.

9) The Star is to make an oral presentation about his/her pictures.

10) Each student is to write a positive note to the Star.

11) Create a book for the Star of the Week containing all of the student compliments about the Star.

12) The Star is the teacher's assistant during the week. He/she runs errands, is the line leader, etc.

Star of The Week Confirmation Letter

To the Parents of _____,

Your child is going to be our Star of the Week during the week of:_____

To help your child prepare for this week and the special recognition that we are going to give him/her please begin gathering:

- Photos from birth to currently

- Awards, certificates, ribbons, etc.

- Things that your child likes to do such as: hobbies, sports, movies, games, favorite books, favorite places, etc. Each day during his/her special week, he/she will have an opportunity to share at least one of the things with the class.

One of the fun activities that we are going to engage in during the first two weeks of school is to create Dream Collages. These will represent your child's dreams and aspirations. They will include such things as places where he/she would like to go, careers that he/she would like to enter, changes that he/she would like to see on earth, what his/her dream home, bedroom, dining room, and game room would look like, and words that may describe him/her in the future, etc.

You may want to begin collecting newspapers, magazines, etc., that your child may use to create his/her Dream Collage. His/her collage will be prominently displayed as part of our Star of the Week bulletin board.

Sincerely,

Star of The Week Reminder Letter

To the Parents of _____,

In our classroom we have a very special bulletin board entitled, "The Spotlight is on You." It is special because it tells about a student in our class and displays pictures of him/her growing up.

Next week is _____ turn to bring in an autobiography and photos of himself/herself growing up. The following are some ideas you may like to include in the autobiography.

1. Date and place of birth
2. Family members
3. Things your child enjoys doing at home.
4. Pets
5. "Future Me" (When I grow up I'd like to be. . .)
6. Favorite foods
7. Favorite TV programs
8. Special friends and and what they like to do together.
9. Favorite sport or activity
10. Trips taken

If possible, please mount your pictures on paper and label them so they can be easily attached to the bulletin board. All items will be returned to you after they have been displayed.

I hope you will enjoy working with your child on this project.

Sincerely,

Activity 11

Words to Live By

Objectives

- To create visual images of words, concepts, and phrases that support and reinforce classroom values.
- To expand vocabulary.
- To nurture self esteem and positive self images.
- To focus on individual behavior.
- To establish a language-behavior association.
- To provide visual images of important character values to be discussed and reinforced during the school year.

Materials

- <u>The Eagles who Thought They were Chickens</u> book and Student Activity book.
- Construction paper.
- Sign board
- Scissors.
- Hole puncher.
- String.

The Eagles who Thought They were Chickens activity has proven very powerful with children in grades K through 12, but especially so in elementary school. All grade levels understand and internalize the behavior of the characters, and are able to engage in dialogue about how certain behavior in school at-large and in individual classrooms are reflective of the behavior of the various characters in the story. Students reason that those who bully, criticize, put down, and ridicule others embody the behavior of the chickens and roosters. Children who have positive attitudes, who are supportive of their classmates, and who are willing to risk failure by trying to spread their wings are recognized as internalizing the behavior of the eagles who found the courage to fly.

Children begin to understand the language-behavior association and literally begin to spread their wings exhibiting eagle behavior:

"Matt, what type of behavior did you exhibit by pushing Ashley?"

"That was chicken behavior Mrs. Blassie."

"Well, Matt what would be eagle behavior?"

"I should not be in a hurry and I should have asked Ashley if I could help her with her things."

"Matt, what would an eagle do when he or she behaves like a chicken?"

"Since I am an eagle I should apologize to Ashley, Mrs. Blassie."

"Thank you, Matt. Okay class, let's go to lunch."

By utilizing a story, anecdote, or poem to facilitate your discussion regarding character values, how we should treat each other, how to have the courage to try, how to use positive and encouraging eagle and Dream-Building words, you engage a number of different learning styles. Student comprehension is substantially increased as many children, in fact, learn best through stories, anecdotes, and poems.

A classroom represents a family. As such, the classroom family develops values, language, behavior, and a way of dealing with conflicts based upon what is being modeled in the family. Word lists provide valuable visual aides for students to focus on during discussions regarding conflicts and how we treat each other, as well as expand their vocabularies with the substance of the personal character that will carry them toward achieving their dreams and aspirations.

Procedure:

1) Each day, use a different word and discuss what it means.

2) "How can we demonstrate today's word in our lives?"

3) "How have we witnessed this word being demonstrated by one of our classmates?"

4) "What character traits are embodied within the character of the story that we're discussing?"

5) "If the character had demonstrated other character traits, how could the story have ended differently?"

6) "What character traits are important to effectively resolving conflicts?"

7) Discuss the character traits or values that have been violated as a result of a particular conflict in your classroom.

Example:

"There was a student who found some money in the classroom and gave it to me. I acknowledged the student and asked the classroom what character values had been demonstrated?"

As a result of this continuous dialogue and focus, all of my students are aware of the character values, as well as the Eagle Words and Dream-Building Words. They can recall most of the words by memory, define each word, and tell you why they are important to society.

Throughout the school year you will witness students becoming more caring and respectful of one another. They are eager to cooperate. When a student is struggling everyone wants to help that student. They internalize the message: we are a **caring dream-building** classroom. We want to assist anyone who needs help.

8) Write the words individually on various visuals and post around the room:

- Bricks for building dreams.
- Clouds, stars, etc. for suspending from the ceiling.
- Flowers for your field of dreams.
- Steps to success.

9) Display prominently in the classroom.

10) Discuss a different character value, eagle, or dream-building word each day.

Expectations are the keys to unlocking the dreams and aspirations buried deep inside of us.

Parkway School District has adopted fifteen **Character Values** that are taught and reinforced in all of our schools. The fifteen values that follow are defined in the appendix:

Character Values

Accountability	Honesty	Integrity
Responsibility	Respect for Self	Abstinence
Caring about others	Commitment to family	Equality
Positive work ethic	Respect for others	Justice
Respect for authority	Respect for property	Freedom

In addition to these words and phrases I teach **Eagle Words** from *The Eagles who Thought They were Chickens* curriculum:

Eagle Words

awesome	beautiful	character	compassion
confidence	considerate	courage	courteous
determination	dignity	diligent	encourage
excellent	extraordinary	faith	fantastic
fortitude	helpful	incredible	inspire
integrity	intelligence	justice	kind
loyal	magnificent	marvelous	outstanding
perseverance	persistent	relentless	remarkable
resilient	reverence	self-esteem	strong
stupendous	supportive	tenacious	valiant
wonderful			

I also use such **Dream-Building Words** as:

Dream-Building Words

helpful	strength	tenacity	unyielding	compassion
vision	ethical	reliable	dependable	empowered
fairness	brilliant	honest	trustworthy	commitment
motivated	dedicated			

Eagle words posted at Fourth Ward Elementary School

A wall illustrates our expectations that everyone can internalize our Character Values.

(Top) A bulletin board in Mrs. Finley's class inspires students to soar. (Bottom) Each week students proudly wear their eagle badges as they are encouraged to embody an eagle concept. This week they are demonstrating COURAGE!

Wynn/Blassie • © 1995 Rising Sun Publishing • (800) 524-2813
Building Dreams: Elementary School Edition Teacher's Guide

Activity 12

Inspirational Quotes

Objectives

- To create visual images of words, concepts, and phrases that support and reinforce classroom values and individual character development.

- To expand student knowledge of famous people, quotations, literature, and poetry.

Materials

- Inspirational materials, e.g., books, essays, quotations, poetry, famous sayings, inspirational posters, etc.

This activity, while challenging for some and easy for others, is fun and inspiring for all.

Simply begin gathering books, posters, quotations, poetry, etc., that are inspiring and thought-provoking. Any quotations or poetry that contains your character values, eagle words or dream-building words are a plus.

Photocopy or rewrite quotations and cut paper into various shapes, e.g., clouds, balloons, apples, pumpkins, flowers, bricks or building blocks, etc. and post around the room. On walls, windows, on the floor, suspended from the ceiling, onto desks, etc.

Have a student select a different quote each day to recite to the class.

I use a verse or quote from Mychal Wynn's book of poetry, *Don't Quit,* each day in my classroom. The first stanza from several of my class's most popular verses are listed on the following page.

Building Dreams in music

After creating melodies, students choose a melody from which to create an ABA instrumental composition. After one melody was chosen, students and the teacher composed the music. The chosen melody was used as the program illustration for the Spring Concert. The composition was performed by students who participated in the creative process. The performance was a success. Parents and other community members requested to have the video copied. It was, and all copies were sold!

— Rosetta Dingle, Music Teacher, Felton Laboratory School, Orangeburg, South Carolina

Born To Win

...They all stand before the rising Sun
With a sense of pride that stands the test
That challenges all who dare to dream
To dare become the best

There's a New Day Coming

...No matter how great the journey, or how heavy the load
How steep the mountain, or how rough the road
When your arms grow weary and legs give way
Stop and rest for a moment, it will be okay

Be The Captain of Your Ship

Be the Captain of your ship
and follow your dreams wherever they lead
allow the winds of faith to fill your sail
and be patient as you set your speed

Dare

...Dare to continue
when all around you are quitting
Dare to have faith
when all around you are doubting
Dare to dream
even if no one dreams with you

Be A Winner

...Hold fast to your dreams, as they can come true
When you do the best that you can possibly do
To win you must believe that you will not fail
Perseverance is the breeze that fills your sail

Banners welcome you to Welborn Elementary School where students are encouraged to dream great dreams and to acquire an education so that they may achieve their dreams.

The walls at Welborn Elementary School display words, phrases, and student papers affirming their dreams and aspirations.

Interacting with Parents

Before the school year begins, my bulletin boards are completed and up. As teachers, it's important to be organized to prepare ourselves to become successful. I call all of the parents before school opens to let them know that I am going to prepare their child to become successful.

"I was so excited when I received my class list and I found your child in my class."

I give parents a homework assignment during my first phone call. I ask them to write me a letter about their son or daughter. They can tell me anything they want. Is there anything I need to know? Do they need any special help?

I also tell my parents that they will be hearing from me regularly.

I call the parents back a few days after school has started to re-affirm how excited I am to have their child in my class. I also give them an example of something that I've noticed about their child.

I didn't see birds!

A young girl had worked very diligently on a class project painting a landscape that she was planning to present to her mother. She had illustrated a landscape along the shoreline. She had never gone to the ocean before and was imagining how wonderful it would be to go some day.

She had worked all week on her painting and on Friday afternoon, just as the students were completing their work, the teacher walked by and commented on how beautiful her painting was. However, the teacher commented that she hadn't drawn any birds and took a small brush and made two small lines for birds near the top of her painting.

The young girl took her painting home after class and instead of presenting it to her mother, she threw it under her bed and burst into tears. Her mother came into her room, saw the painting sticking out from under the bed, pulled the painting out, and asked her daughter why she was crying. She commented on how it was such a beautiful painting. The young girl cried as she told her mother about how proud she had been of her painting and how she had planned to present it to her. The young girl continued crying as she pointed at the painting saying, "I didn't see any birds!"

Activity 13

Popsicle Sticks

Objectives

- To provide each student with an opportunity for individual attention and recognition.
- To initiate periodic parental contact.

Materials

- Popsicle sticks.

This activity was passed on to me from Lynn Brengle, a very talented teacher. The activity helps students become self directed in their behavior because they never know when their number will be pulled. All they know is that I am observing a special student each day and that I will share my observations at the end of the day with his/her parent. I find that there is a lot of excitement each day as students guess who it is.

Research demonstrates that one of the most disappointing areas of a child's schooling is never being noticed. We all should have an opportunity to feel special–that someone is paying attention to us all day long just because we are special!

"Each student in my classroom has a number corresponding to a popsicle stick that I keep on my desk. Each morning I pull a popsicle stick at random. I observe the student whose number corresponds to the popsicle stick throughout the day. At 3:15 all of the students are anxious to know whose parent is going to get called that day. Not only are the students excited but they are encouraged to be on their best behavior every day because no one knows whose parents are going to be called!"

"When your child's number is selected, I will call you that evening with a realistic assessment of my observations of your child during the day. This is just one of the ways in which I am trying to help your child become successful."

"Hello, this is Mrs. Blassie. Today is your lucky day. Mychal-David was chosen for an observation in the classroom. I was really excited to see Mychal-David's enthusiasm to help his peers with artist's workshop. He's a very talented artist and is eager to assist others with their artwork."

"Do you have any questions or concerns about Mychal-David's progress at this time?"

"Thanks for being a part of Mrs. Blassie's Dream Team!"

Procedure:

1) Assign each of your students a number.

2) Write the corresponding number on a popsicle stick.

3) Keep the popsicle sticks on your desk in a cup or can.

4) Select a stick at the beginning of each school day and observe the student throughout the day making notes that you can share with their parent(s).

Activity 14

Parent Communication

Objectives

- To quickly and effectively communicate classroom activities, content being covered, and what parents can do to support their child's learning.

- To keep parents informed of what you are doing in class.

Materials

- Preprinted note paper cut into the shapes of the various monthly themes.

A special thanks to Donna Pelikan for sharing her ideas and her "I wish my child's teacher would. . ." letter.

Introduce this activity at open house with a follow up letter the next week to each child regardless of his/her parent attendance at open house. Each Friday an "I wish my child's teacher would. . ." letter will go home that encourages parent communication of their concerns and child's needs with the teacher. Consider copying this onto the reverse side of your weekly letter.

"To best help me prepare your child to become successful I will be sending home notes. These notes will keep you informed of what types of activities we're working on in class, what character words we are discussing, and how you can help to reinforce and possibly expand upon what we're learning in class."

"One of our first activities will be to create 'My Third Grade Portfolio.' Your child will be able to draw, paste pictures, and write things about his or her family, culture, history, and experiences. It may include things about where he/she lives, goes to church, and whatever represents his/her life during the forthcoming school year. We will work on this activity for about a week after which your child will bring his/her portfolio home with his/her first graded assignments."

"The portfolio will be a good place to keep everything that your child brings home relating to their third grade year in school including assignments, notes that I send home, and other important information about the school."

To be more organized, every Friday or every two weeks, staple all papers together with a brief note (see samples). There is a space for the parents to comment. The note must come back signed or call the home.

"Just a note to say how talented Susan is at art and creative projects."

"Just wanted to let you know how proud Mychal-David was today to share his summer activities with the class."

"Just a note to say that Ashley has been helping me organize the class. She'll make a wonderful teacher."

"Just wanted to let you know that Jalani talks about his daddy all of the time."

"Just wanted to let you know that Mark wants to become a hockey player. He just doesn't know that Michael Jordan doesn't play hockey!"

"Just wanted to let you know that Brittany is going to be my special helper next week."

Procedure:

1) Review the "My Portfolio" activity. [Activity 20.]

2) Print your name, classroom, and school telephone number onto master copies of your note paper.

3) Photocopy your note paper and cut into various shapes representing your monthly themes.

4) Place into a conveniently-located box so that you can grab one easily to note various things that you witness in your students.

5) Use these to communicate to parents those "Aha" experiences where a student suddenly gets it, or when a student is supportive or encouraging of a classmate, or when a student is particularly helpful, etc.

If you want a parent to read information:

Send them regular notes saying positive things about their child.

Send home graded work using phrases such as wonderful, gifted, shows particular insight, marvelous, great, really worked hard, fantastic, clearly demonstrates that he has learned, demonstrates remarkable understanding and comprehension, is excelling beyond expectations, has demonstrated remarkable improvement, she's destined to become a Ph.D. in science or nuclear physics, wow!

Write it in bright red and put a star on it.

Children love to see their names attached to such comments: Great Lauren, Super Ashley, Marvelous Mychal-David, Magnificent Matt, Jolly Jalani.

Send parents occasional notes saying, "Thank you for your support."

Send the important papers that you wish parents to review and return in a special folder which has a "please return by" date on it.

If you don't get it by the due date, call the parent.

Date: _____

From the Parents of: _____

I wish my child's teacher would . . .

From: _____   Date: _____

Grade: _____

_____
_____
_____
_____

Things To Say To Your Children To Help Them Discover Their Dreams and Aspirations

wow, you're so good at that • you really have a special gift for that • that's outstanding, how would you like to learn more about that? • that's remarkable, I'll bet that few people would have done it that way • you like that so much, maybe we could see if there are any special schools or camps where you could learn more about that • you're on your way to becoming a great. . . • let's go to the library and see how much we can find out about that • there's a story about someone who's doing what you want to do. Let's write them a letter and ask them how they got started • I picked up something special for you today that would help you to become a. . . • let's see if there are any books or magazines about that • let's ask you teacher if she can help you learn more about doing that • let's create a portfolio so that we can save your work • hi, this is my son. He's going to become a great. . . • hi, this is my daughter. She has an extraordinary talent for. . . • let's go and see a movie about that • let's see how many books we can find about that • let's create a special place where we can display your work*

© Rising Sun Publishing (800) 524-2813

From: _____ Date: _____

Grade: _____

_____
_____
_____
_____

Things To Do To Reinforce Children's Talents and Interests

go to the library with them • praise them • allow them to move at their own pace • tell others about how proud you are of their talents and interests without embarrassing them • introduce them to others with similar talents and interests • be supportive without being pushy • don't compare what they like to do to with what you would like them to like to do • provide opportunities for them to experience, create, experiment, and expand their talents and interests • never attempt to motivate through ridicule • allow them space to explore, attempt, fail, change, and pursue their heart's desires • if they're competitive help them to develop a positive and healthy spirit, if they're not competitive don't force them to compete • allow them to have their own dreams and aspirations • don't attempt to live your dreams through them!

© Rising Sun Publishing (800) 524-2813

From: _____   Date: _____

Grade: _____

_____

_____

_____

_____

101 Ways To Praise Your Child

wow • way to go • super • you're special • outstanding • excellent • great • good • neat • well done • remarkable • I knew you could do it • I'm proud of you • fantastic • superstar • nice work • looking good • you're on top of it • beautiful • now you're flying • you're catching on • now you're got it • you're incredible • bravo • you're fantastic • hurray for you • you're on target • you're on your way • how nice • how smart • good job • that's incredible • hot dog • dynamite • you're beautiful • you're unique • nothing can stop you now • good for you • I like you • you're a winner • remarkable job • beautiful work • spectacular • you're spectacular • you're darling • you're precious • great discovery • you've discovered the secret • you figured it out • fantastic job • hip, hip hurray • bingo • magnificent • marvelous • terrific • you're important • phenomenal • you're sensational • super work • creative job • super job • fantastic job • exceptional performance

© Rising Sun Publishing (800) 524-2813

Activity 15

Making Parents Feel Welcomed

Objectives

- To solicit greater parental involvement.

- To communicate to your students the shared partnership in preparing them to become successful.

- To free up more time for professional development, teaching, and dealing with the unique needs of the classroom.

Materials

- Laminated apples that will serve as name tags for parents.

- Permanent-ink black markers.

- Straight pins.

- A box where everything can be stored in a permanent place, easily accessible to parents.

During the first phone call, encourage all parents to volunteer in class. Outline for parents the areas they can support in the classroom. Create a folder for each parent with their names on it so when they come into class they don't interrupt the lesson. All directions are placed in their folders: tutoring a student in math, reading, etc., filing, correcting tests or organizing papers, getting projects ready, reading to a small group or supervising a learning center.

"To best help me help your child to become successful, I recruit classroom helpers to help me during or after class. Classroom helpers consist of parents, grandparents, volunteers, retired teachers, Mentors, older brothers or sisters, or anyone who wants to see your child learn and have a successful school year."

"I'm going to need help putting together a monthly calendar of classroom volunteers. I've put together a sheet of the areas that I need help with, however, feel free to help in any way you can. Also feel free to recruit grandparents, aunts, uncles, or anyone whom you trust and whom you believe could be an asset to our class."

Procedure:

1) Prepare a list of those areas where you could benefit from parental involvement (see the list on the following page).

2) Distribute the list to each parent.

I recommend that we have a listening day each week, during which time we listen to the students, not, I hasten to say, the plain or distorted echoes of ourselves. We might be surprised at what the kids have to tell us. Teach Us What We Want to Know, the published findings of the Connecticut State Board of Education's research program to redesign their health curriculum, is an instructive insight into the real world of the child's mind. . . Were teachers to spend more time in honest listening and noncomitant honest exploration, perhaps the classroom would be a place where our children would more gladly go.

— Henry F. Beechhold, *The Creative Classroom*

Dear Parent,

During the week of _____

We will be working on the following activities:

_____
_____
_____
_____
_____

You can reinforce what the children are learning in class by:

_____
_____
_____
_____
_____

Sincerely,

Student: _____

Parent: _____

Hm phone: _____

Wk phone: _____

Please check all that apply:

- ☐ Will make learning games
- ☐ Will help with classroom crafts/projects
- ☐ Will type children's stories on computer
- ☐ Will grade papers
- ☐ Will chaperone field trips
- ☐ Will help with guest speakers
- ☐ Will lead a special interest group(s)

_____

- ☐ I have a special hobby that I will share:

_____
_____

Building Dreams: Elementary School Edition © 1995 RISING SUN PUBLISHING (800) 524-2813

Student: _____

Parent: _____

Hm phone: _____ Wk phone: _____

This is a list of things we need in our classroom. Please check/circle all that apply:

☐ I can provide some supplies (paper, pencils, glue, paper clips, etc.)

☐ I am available to read to students.
    once a week   twice a week   once a month   more

☐ I am available to tutor reading.
    once a week   twice a week   once a month   more

☐ I am available to tell stories.
    once a week   twice a week   once a month   more

☐ I am available to grade papers.
    once a week   twice a week   once a month   more

☐ I am available to help in the classroom.
    once a week   twice a week   once a month   more

☐ I am interested in helping with projects such as:

Science   Social Studies   Dream Building   Math   Book Club   Art   Computer Guest speakers   Putting up classroom displays   Other

☐ I am available to read to my child at home.

☐ I am available to help my child with homework.

☐ I am willing to tutor students after school.

☐ I am willing to work on dream-building activities such as getting speakers, gathering information, facilitating special days and field trips, etc. and doing whatever is needed to help our children's dreams become a reality.

Activity 16

The First Day of School

Objectives

- To get off to a positive start.

- To ease the natural anxieties that students experience on the first day of school.

- To immediately familiarize students with classroom procedures and your expectations.

- To bond with students while contributing to individual self esteem.

Materials

- Construction paper.
- Scissors.
- Markers.

The first and most frightening thing on a student's mind is, "Am I in the right room?" In some large school settings, the classroom may be the safest place in the minds of many students as they cope with all of the different anxieties of returning to school, going to school for the first time, going to a new school, or moving into a new community–not to mention the anxiety of many students at simply meeting the teacher. As the classroom teacher, you have the power to help your students make a smooth transition.

"I'd like to welcome all of you here to our classroom where we're going to help each other to become successful this year. However first, we want to make sure that everyone is in the correct room. Look around the room at the stars that are posted on the walls and when you see your name quietly raise your hand."

"You'll notice that each star tells us a little about each of our classmates. We're going to learn a lot more about each other this year as we work together."

Procedure:

1) Create an illustrative sign to post outside of your classroom. Indicate your name, room number, grade level, subject (if appropriate), and a greeting or classroom slogan.

2) Below the sign post a list of the students in your class.

3) Post the same information from your outside sign inside your classroom on the board.

4) Post the student stars around the classroom. Each star should have the student's full name, and something that he/she likes to do or an area of achievement.

Example:

Mychal-David Wynn is a black belt in Karate.

Lauren Smith loves performing in plays.

5) Stand at the door and greet each student. Give them a hug or handshake and a smile as they enter the classroom.

6) If you have assigned seating, tell the students as they enter the classroom how to find their seats.

Example:

"Good morning, Mychal-David. You can find your desk by looking for your name in the top right-hand corner. Do you think that you can find it okay? If you have a problem, come back and tell me, okay?"

7) Have an assignment on each student's desk. Tell them as they come into the classroom that you would like for them to complete the assignment as soon as they sit down. Make the assignment a puzzle, word game, or other activity that they will find interesting while other students are entering the classroom.

8) Begin by asking questions about the assignment. Compliment students for their answers and use their responses to lead you into discussing your procedural charts. Begin with the chart of "How to answer questions."

9) Spend the day discussing the various procedures in the classroom and why the students are responsible for knowing them.

10) Walk around the room and discuss each procedural chart and each bulletin board.

11) Ask students why they think these are important.

In <u>Punished by Rewards</u>, Alfie Kohn notes the importance of structuring an environment in which students can explore, make mistakes, acknowledge when they don't know, and risk failing without risk of ridicule from teacher or their peers:

. . .a classroom that feels safe to students is one in which they are free to admit when they don't understand something and are able to ask for help. Ironically, grades and tests, punishments and rewards, are the enemies of safety; they therefore reduce the probability that students will speak up and that truly productive evaluation can take place.

. . .for parents, it means first of all thinking carefully about one's motives for pushing children to get better grades. After reading the evidence and weighing the arguments, it makes sense for parents to consider putting aside grades and scores as indicators of success and to look instead at the child's *interest* in learning. This is the primary criterion by which schools (and our own actions) should be judged.

Welcome mistakes. Mistakes are our friends, announces a sign seen on some classroom walls. Experienced teachers watch and listen closely for when students get things wrong. They don't become defensive, because they know mistakes don't necessarily reflect poor teaching. They don't become angry, because they know mistakes don't necessarily reflect sloppiness or laziness. (If they do, the challenge is to figure out why a student is being sloppy or lazy and work together to solve the problem.) Mistakes offer information about how a student thinks. Correcting them quickly and efficiently doesn't do much to facilitate the learning process. More important, students who are afraid of making mistakes are unlikely to ask for help when they need it, unlikely to feel safe enough to take intellectual risks, and unlikely to be intrinsically motivated.

Activity 17

Greeting Students with TLC

Objectives

- To provide each student with at least one positive and loving person in his/her school day.

- To help parents help their children.

- To help each student feel that he/she is loved.

Materials

- Perfume or Cologne.

- Mouthwash or breath mints.

- Extra toothbrushes and toothpaste.

I explain to parents that sometimes in our busy lives and in the lives of our children, we begin some days the wrong way. And, that if their child finds himself/herself experiencing a bad day, they can call the school and have a note placed in my box asking that I give their child some extra TLC (tender loving care) that day. The parent doesn't have to tell me why or what, specifically, is wrong. They only need to let me know that their child needs some special attention that day.

In response to the parent's request, I may point out something special to their child: "Justin, will you come here? Could you please do something for me?" or, "Hi, I like what you have on today," or, "I really like the way you came into class quietly today."

As society changes; as more Americans become homeless; as more children enter foster, adoptive, and extended family care; as more families lose loved ones, their jobs, and homes; as more students are abused or witness abuse; and as more of our children become the victims or perpetrators of violence, we are challenged with giving even more of ourselves.

For some children, your love may be the only love they receive that day. Your smile may be the only genuine, caring, and comforting smile they receive that day. The meals served in school may be the only nutritious meals they will receive that day. What happens in your classroom may be the only hope that your students have for a brighter tomorrow.

Preparing our children for the opportunities of life relates directly to our expectations. Where we expect failure, we allow for failure. Where we expect success, we prepare for success.

— Mychal Wynn, *Building Dreams: Helping Students Discover Their Potential*

Purpose:

1) To welcome each student to a place of learning, caring, nurturing, and support.

2) To help parents to feel that their children are safe with you and that you are concerned about their mental health.

3) To defuse situations before they start by helping those who may have gotten off to a bad start to walk into a better day.

4) To bond with students so that you can more effectively mediate and resolve future conflicts.

Procedure:

1) Keep perfume or cologne, mouthwash or breath freshener in your classroom.

2) Be sure that you smell good each day before your students come into class.

3) Greet each student at the door. I hug all of my students, but that's a function of personality. Do what you feel comfortable with as long as you greet each one individually.

4) Give yourself a little spritz of perfume and breath freshener after lunch.

5) Get into the habit of complimenting each of your students. Keep a log book to ensure that you compliment each student at least three times per week.

6) Remember: There will be days when you don't want to smile, but fake it until you make it!

Self-esteem. While social learning is important in positive families, so too is respect for the individual. Parents in these families help cultivate self-esteem by providing frequent opportunities for self-expression and self-actualization. Praise is used not as a behavioral pellet to reward acceptable performance but as a natural outcome of joy at seeing an individual realize his potential. Regular time is taken in these families to acknowledge and validate each person's inner experience. All family members have a chance to talk about or demonstrate special abilities and accomplishments and to feel affirmed by their achievements as well as by their very existence.

— Thomas Armstrong, *Awakening Your Child's Natural Genius*

Activity 18

Classy Compliment Tree

Objectives

- To provide a visual aide for focusing students on successful behavior.
- To help students focus on each others' good qualities.
- To help students reinforce positive behavior among their peers.
- To help raise individual student self esteem.
- To help students learn how to compliment others.

Materials

- Construction paper.
- Scissors.
- Note paper.

I model the desired behavior for the first two weeks of school. I make compliments regarding the behavior, support, encouragement, work habits, and positive attitudes of students. I write down the compliments onto little apples, and I post them on the Classy Compliment Tree noting the name of the person being complimented and the person paying the compliment.

Students go out of their way to do things during the two weeks that I model this. Afterwards, students can write a compliment about themselves or about someone else.

I observe the students, and as I notice dream behavior, I write it down and tack it on the wall. At the end of the day, I read all the compliments to the children and share my delight in their dream behavior. Of course, this is contagious: And after I use it as a role model, after two weeks, the children take the responsibility over. They love it!!

Procedure:

1) Whenever you see a student doing something nice or responsibly following a procedure, write down a compliment about that student.

2) Each month, create a different cut-out representing that month's theme (e.g., first month of school use an apple; in October use pumpkins; in November use turkeys; etc.).

Example:

Amie needed a pencil and Renee gave her one. "I like the way Renee shared a pencil with Amie."

John was absent and Robert offered to take John his assignment. "I like the way Robert went out of his way to see that John received his assignments. Robert wanted to help John to become successful."

Dear Mrs. Blassie,

What I liked about our class was how you wanted to know about our dreams. You tried to help us to succeed and to make our dreams come true.

I don't think you should change anything. Our class has Dream words, Character Values, and the Classy Compliment Tree. Those things are all great!

I think you should continue the Dream Team, the Classy Compliment Tree, and the Character Values.

Sincerely,

Beth Lewis [Third grade student]

Mychal Wynn and Dee Blassie stand in front of the Classy Compliment Tree as they talk with students about what it takes to achieve your dreams.

Mrs. Blassie encourages students to Fall Into Good Habits through her various procedural charts which outline responsible behavior.

Wynn/Blassie • © 1995 Rising Sun Publishing • (800) 524-2813
Building Dreams: Elementary School Edition Teacher's Guide

Who You Are Makes A Difference

A teacher in New York decided to honor each of her seniors in high school by telling them the difference they each made. Using a process developed by Helice Bridges of Del Mar, California, she called each student to the front of the class, one at a time. First she told them how the student made a difference to her and the class. Then she presented each of them with a blue ribbon imprinted with gold letters which read, "Who I Am Makes a Difference."

Afterwards the teacher decided to do a class project to see what kind of impact recognition would have on a community. She gave each of the students three more ribbons and instructed them to go out and spread this acknowledgment ceremony.

One of the boys in the class went to a junior executive in a nearby company and honored him for helping him with his career planning. He gave him a blue ribbon and put it on his shirt. Then he gave him two extra ribbons, and said, "We're doing a class project on recognition, and we'd like you to go out, find somebody to honor, give them a blue ribbon, then give them the extra blue ribbon so they can acknowledge a third person."

Later that day the junior executive went in to see his boss, who had been noted, by the way, as being kind of a grouchy fellow. He sat his boss down and he told him that he deeply admired him for being a creative genius. The boss seemed very surprised. The junior executive asked him if he would accept the gift of the blue ribbon and would he give him permission to put it on him. His surprised boss said, "Well, sure."

The junior executive took the blue ribbon and placed it right on his boss's jacket above his heart. As he gave him the last extra ribbon, he said, "Would you do me a favor? Would you take this extra ribbon and pass it on by honoring somebody else?"

That night the boss came home to his 14-year-old son and sat him down. He said, "The most incredible thing happened to me today. He shared what had happened with his son and went on to say, "As I was driving home tonight, I started thinking about whom I would honor with this ribbon and I thought about you. I want to honor you."

"My days are really hectic and when I come home I don't pay a lot of attention to you. Sometimes I scream at you for not getting good enough grades in school and for your bedroom being a mess, but somehow tonight, I just wanted to sit here and, well, just let you know that you do make a difference to me. Besides your mother, you are the most important person in my life. You're a great kid and I love you!"

The startled boy started to sob and sob, and he couldn't stop crying. His whole body shook. He looked up at his father and said through his tears, "I was planning on committing suicide tomorrow, Dad, because I didn't think you loved me. Now I don't need to."

— Helice Bridges, in *Chicken Soup for the Soul*

Activity 19

Fight-Free/Conflict-Free Bulletin Board

Objectives

- To provide a visual aide for focusing students on successful behavior.

- To formally recognize students who exhibit desired behavior.

- To provide students with a behavioral goal that can be realized and validated in front of their peers.

- To focus attention on students who need greater support from the classroom community.

Materials

- Construction paper.
- Scissors.
- Border.
- Ribbon.
- Name tags.

Special thanks Peggy Dolan, principal of McNair School, Hazelwood School District, St. Louis, Missouri, for sharing such a wonderful activity. This activity is part of a larger program that Peggy has created called "The Fight-Free Schools Program," which is currently being implemented in 26 states, South Africa, and Nova Scotia.

"To promote a peaceful dream classroom where we all can focus our energy on learning instead of conflicts, we will celebrate every Friday by proudly wearing our fight-free ribbons. In addition, our big fight free ribbon for the class is proudly displayed on our classroom door [or fight-free bulletin board] to let everyone know that we have been fight free all week!"

"An award will be given monthly to all students who have demonstrated the Dream Team Spirit!"

Although our class went throughout the entire school year virtually fight-free, one day a conflict occurred. Two students had a conflict and were sent to Mr. Sainz, the principal. During the five minutes or so that they were waiting, Ginny Altrogge, the assistant principal, came in and they told her that they had to learn to get along with each other and that they had learned that two of the character values are to be honest and responsible. "So we want to be responsible for our actions and be honest with you to let you know that we both are in the wrong!" They were about to resolve their differences without adult intervention!

Procedure:

1) Every student has a name tag and ribbon that hangs on the board.

2) Students who have been fight-free [or conflict-free] throughout the week are allowed to wear their ribbons on Friday.

3) Classroom conflicts are encouraged to be resolved as a family, in a manner consistent with our character values.

4) If the entire class has been fight-free [or conflict-free] have a class ceremony to post the class ribbon outside on the classroom door.

5) Have a monthly celebration.

Activity 20

My Portfolio

Objectives

- To begin the school year with an activity that celebrates the culture, families, and communities of each student.

- To help students appreciate positive things about themselves and their families.

- To provide parents with a convenient tool for storage of their child's work, activities, and school-related information.

Materials

- Construction paper.
- Poster board.
- Magazines/newspapers.
- Family photos.
- Scissors.
- Glue.

In this activity, we are going to engage students in looking at their year in school. The completed portfolio, folder, crate, or box will be sent home to parents at the beginning of the school year so that they will have a convenient place to store their child's work and other school-related information. This will also help parents to conveniently track their child's progress and to prepare questions for the periodic parent-teacher conferences.

Please join in this activity with your students. Create your own portfolio. You can collect special pictures, shared moments, notes about students and notes about your colleagues. Wouldn't it be great to go back to your kindergarten teacher and see the notes he or she made about you that have been saved all these years in a portfolio?

My Third Grade Portfolio

"Class we are going to work on creating a project this week called 'My Third Grade Portfolio.' When we've completed our portfolios, we're going to display them and then take them home and give them to our parents. Your parents can keep all of your school assignments, information regarding the school, and other work that you may take home during the school year."

"To create our portfolios, we are going to take a picture of everyone in our class so that our pictures can go onto our portfolios. I also would like for you to bring to school a newspaper representing one day this week. For example, if your parents have today's paper or can buy tomorrow's paper, bring the paper to school so that you can paste the date from the paper together with articles about life in *your town* during your first week of school."

"You may also bring photos of your house, family, church, community, relatives, or places that you went this past summer."

Preparation:

1) Prepare working areas for students.

2) Gather all materials (glue, scissors, markers, paints, etc.).

Note:

If you are going to use crates or boxes, ask parents at Open House to send a box or crate with a lid that they can purchase from stores like K-Mart® or Wal-Mart®.

Procedure:

1) Organize student work areas.

2) Lay out two large sheets of poster board (or use a box) for each student. Note that the poster board should be oblong. Once completed, the poster boards will be stapled together along the sides and bottoms lengthwise to create an open envelope.

3) Have students lay out their photos, date from the newspaper, newspaper articles, etc.

4) Have students write (onto separate paper and cut out) or cut out the letters directly from construction paper, MY THIRD GRADE YEAR IN SCHOOL.

5) Have them position their letters onto one poster board and glue into position.

6) Have them position their photos, newspaper date, newspaper articles, etc., onto each of the boards [one side only] and glue into position when they are satisfied.

The dreams of our children provides the "hook" from which we can reel them into our schools and classrooms. A person's dream of becoming, dream of doing, dream of changing, dream of performing, dream of inventing, dream of seeing, dream of knowing, or dream of discovering, gives them a purpose for being. It is this purpose and direction that becomes the driving force behind their desire for learning.

— Mychal Wynn, _Building Dreams: Helping Students Discover Their Potential_

For all our talk about motivation, I think we often fail to recognize a truth that is staring us in the face: if educators are able to create the conditions under which children can become engaged with academic tasks, the acquisition of intellectual skills will probably follow. We want students to become rigorous thinkers, accomplished readers and writers and problem solvers who can make connections and distinctions between ideas. But the most reliable guide to a process that is promoting these things is not grades or tests scores: it is the student's level of interests.

— Alfie Kohn, _Punished by Rewards_

Activity 21

Gathering Information About Your Students

Objectives

- To solicit greater parental involvement.

- To get parents thinking about the resources they have that can help their child.

- To gain insight into the amount of at-home support available to each child.

Materials

- Family information forms (printed on the following pages).

I let all of my parents know that I need help preparing their children to become successful. If they want to come into the classroom and help, or if they want to come into the classroom and work with their child or other children one-on-one, they're welcomed. I encourage volunteers.

I offer them an opportunity to come in and read to students, grade papers, work with groups of students, etc.

My children see parents and grandparents in our classroom and feel that it is a safe environment. In addition, they know someone cares.

"To best help me prepare your child to become successful I would like you to share with me anything that will help me get to know your child and the uniqueness of his or her situation better."

"It's going to be impossible for me to get to know as much as I would like to about each student in my classroom this year without your help and input."

"If there is any information you feel is of a personal nature, simply skip over it. No explanation is necessary. I only want information that you feel comfortable sharing."

"I realize that some of the questions such as whether you have a photocopier or FAX machine at home may seem silly; however, the only way for me to understand the complete scope of the resources available to our classroom is to ask."

Preparation:

1) Send the packet of information to your students' homes before school or prepare the accompanying packet of information so that you can personally hand out to each parent when they attend the very first parent meeting—often the first day of school.

2) Distribute to each parent and ask that they return it by the end of the first week of school or at the open house if you can send it to them in advance. Use this opportunity to remind them to write you a letter describing their child if they have not already returned it.

3) Include your list of student supplies and other pertinent information.

Dear Parent,

Throughout the school year, I will work to keep you informed about what we're working on in class, things that I'm noticing about your child such as the way he/she is relating to other children, how he/she is managing his/her time and completing assignments, how actively he/she is participating in classroom discussions and activities, and anything about his/her personality or learning style that I think might be helpful information for you.

To best help me communicate with you I've attached a brief questionnaire.

When completing the questionnaire, please list the parents' names in the order of first contact. For example: father first or mother first. Indicate whether you would prefer that I contact you during the day or during the evening and during what hours.

Also indicate whether you have a preference of an evening conference or a conference during the school day.

In our classroom we work very hard to help children discover their dreams and aspirations. We believe that this is important in helping children to understand how what they're learning in school is relevant to achieving their dreams and aspirations in life. One of our first activities is to get to know the students who make up our classroom family. You can help us by attaching a photo to the sheet entitled "I Dream Of. . ." by completing a biographical sketch telling about your child's dreams and aspirations, hobbies, special interests, places where he/she would like to go, things that he/she would like to do, etc.

My conference time is: _____

My planning time is: _____

You may contact me during these times at: _____

Sincerely,

I Dream Of . . .

_____

_____

_____

_____

_____

_____

_____

_____

_____

_____

_____

_____

© Rising Sun Publishing (800) 524-2813

Date: _____

Dear Parent,

Enclosed are copies of our classroom procedures. Please go over them with your child. We have discussed all of the procedures in class and your child should be able to explain the procedures to you.

After you have reviewed the procedures with your child please sign below and return this note to school.

_____

Parent's signature   Date

Over a period of years, with Mother's constant encouragement, both Curtis and I started believing that we really could do anything we choose to do. Maybe she brainwashed us into believing that we were going to be extremely good and highly successful at whatever we attempted. Even today I can clearly hear her voice in the back of my head saying, "Bennie, you can do it. Don't you stop believing that for one second."

An excerpt from *Gifted Hands*, a book about the life of Ben Carson, who went from being the dumbest kid in his fifth grade class to becoming the first surgeon to successfully separate siamese twins connected at the brain.

© Rising Sun Publishing (800) 524-2813

Student: _____
_____

Parent/guardian: _____
Home phone: _____
Work phone: _____
_____

I prefer that you call me at home during the hours of:
_____

I prefer that you call me at work during the hours of:
_____

Parent/guardian: _____
Home phone: _____
Work phone: _____
_____

I prefer that you call me at home during the hours of:
_____

I prefer that you call me at work during the hours of:
_____

The best time for an at-school conference is:
    Morning   Afternoon   Evening

Building Dreams: Elementary School Edition © 1995 RISING SUN PUBLISHING (800) 524-2813

Dear Parent(s),

I am really excited about having your child in my class this school year. I'm looking forward to having a wonderful year in which the students learn as much as they can in a classroom environment that encourages them to try hard without fear of failing.

To best help me help your child I would like for you to share with me anything that will help me get to know your child and the uniqueness of his or her situation better. It's going to be impossible for me to get to know as much as I would like to about each student in my classroom this year without your help and input.

If there is any information on the forms that I've enclosed that you feel is of a personal nature, simply skip over it. No explanation is necessary. I only want the information that you feel comfortable about sharing.

I realize that some of the questions such as whether you have a photocopier or FAX machine at home may seem silly, however, the only way for me to understand the complete scope of the resources available to our students is to ask.

Please return this information to me by: _____

Also, tell me one thing that your child really likes to do, or eat, or place to go, or an achievement that he or she is really proud of. I'm going to write each student's name together with their "special something" and post these around the room.

Sincerely,

Student: _____

Parents: _____

Hm phone: _____

Wk phone: _____

The following information is only to help me better understand your child and his/her family. If you feel any question is too personal, you do not need to answer. This information is only to help me best help your child.

My child's parent(s) is/are:

Single   Married   Separated   Divorced   Widow(er)

Grand Parent   Aunt/Uncle   Older Sister/Brother

My child gets to school by:

School bus   walking   I drop him/her off   He/she shares a ride

Other: _____

My child takes the following medications: _____
_____

My child:

Has own room   Shares/1 person   Shares/2 or more

My child goes to bed at: _____

My child wakes up at: _____

My child has breakfast before school: *Yes   No*

Other Comments: _____
_____
_____

Building Dreams: Elementary School Edition © 1995 RISING SUN PUBLISHING (800) 524-2813

Student: _____

At-home Resources

- ☐ Desk and Chair
- ☐ Quiet, well-lighted study area
- ☐ Designated Study Time
- ☐ Help with homework
- ☐ Books (circle)   1-10   11-20   21-30   31-40   40 +
- ☐ Supplies (pencils, crayons, paper, etc.)
- ☐ Television
- ☐ Daily Newspaper
- ☐ VCR
- ☐ Tape Recorder
- ☐ Professional or trade magazines
- ☐ Dictionary
- ☐ Encyclopedias
- ☐ Study Partner
- ☐ Personal Computer
- ☐ Macintosh Computer
- ☐ Printer
- ☐ Photo Copier
- ☐ FAX Machine
- ☐ CD ROM
- ☐ Internet or on-line service
- ☐ Other (describe)

Building Dreams: Elementary School Edition © 1995 RISING SUN PUBLISHING (800) 524-2813

Student: _____

What my child does after school

1. _____
_____

2. _____
_____

3. _____
_____

4. _____
_____

5. _____
_____

6. _____
_____

7. _____
_____

8. _____
_____

9. _____
_____

Building Dreams: Elementary School Edition © 1995 RISING SUN PUBLISHING (800) 524-2813

Student: _____

What I know about my child's personality

Works well alone:
   Always   *Often*   *Sometimes*   *Rarely*

Works well with other children:
   Always   *Often*   *Sometimes*   *Rarely*

Needs personal attention:
   Always   *Often*   *Sometimes*   *Rarely*

Expresses positive feelings and emotions:
   Always   *Often*   *Sometimes*   *Rarely*

Expresses anger:
   Always   *Often*   *Sometimes*   *Rarely*

Enjoys schoolwork:
   Always   *Often*   *Sometimes*   *Rarely*

Is easily distracted:
   Always   *Often*   *Sometimes*   *Rarely*

Enjoys talking while working:
   Always   *Often*   *Sometimes*   *Rarely*

Enjoys eating or snacking while working:
   Always   *Often*   *Sometimes*   *Rarely*

Enjoys crafts/working with his/her hands:
   Always   *Often*   *Sometimes*   *Rarely*

Is easily influenced by others:
   Always   *Often*   *Sometimes*   *Rarely*

Other: _____

Building Dreams: Elementary School Edition © 1995 RISING SUN PUBLISHING (800) 524-2813

Activity 22

Why I Come To School

Objectives

- To understand your students better.

- To help students think about why they come to school and what types of things they should be learning.

- To assess at the beginning and again at the end of the school year how children view their school experience.

Materials

- None required.

Children have many different reasons for attending school. In elementary school the reasons can range from receiving free lunch to being in love with their teachers. Some children view school as a safe environment while others only come because their parents won't allow them to stay at home.

This is a beginning of the year activity that is repeated at the end of the year. What students tell us will help us to evaluate what cannot be readily tested: attitude toward school and learning. We are likely to find a correlation between attitude toward school and academic achievement. Interestingly, many schools experience student attitudes changing regarding school as they enter fifth grade. Many students become less interested and more rebellious with some experiencing declines in academic achievement that continues into Middle School. However, few schools ask children during these difficult years, "Why do you come to school?"

"Class, we're going to do an activity where we're going to write a one-page paper about why we come to school. There are no right or wrong answers. We want to be honest. There are some people who love to come to school for a variety of reasons. For example PE, art, or because they like their teachers. I remember that there were days that I didn't want to go to school, but my mother made the best lunches. I used to go to school just so that my mother could make me one of those wonderful lunches."

"Take your time and think for a moment 'Why do I come to school?' Is it simply because my parents won't let me stay at home?"

To take students from many inner-city backgrounds, or any other background, and attempt to teach without explaining what's in it for them is pretty much like putting a Band-Aid on a hemorrhage. Students must first be taught to like themselves, and each day must serve as a convincing factor of the things that they can do "right." Few of us can sustain a relationship in which everything we do is wrong and we are always told what is wrong with us. This is why we never say to a student, "This is wrong." We always say, "Good try, let's proofread this or that." The word "proofread," to me, sounds better than the word "wrong."

— Marva Collins, *Ordinary Children, Extraordinary Teachers*

Activity 23

Personality Types

Objectives

- To help each student identify his/her unique personality type and gain an appreciation of the various personality types represented in the classroom.

- To gather background information that will help in establishing cooperative groups.

- To help identify personal strengths that could be applied toward particular dreams and aspirations.

Materials

- Personality Type sheets.

"Each of us has a special and unique personality. Our personality reflects how we like to do things, what types of things we like to do, and the situations in which we feel most comfortable."

"For example, raise your hand if you do your homework while listening to the radio or watching TV. Now, raise you hand if you prefer that it is quiet when you do your homework. Raise your hand if you prefer working in large groups. How about small groups? How about working alone? Raise your hand if you like having a lot of friends. How about just a few friends?"

"There's a lot for us to learn about ourselves and about each other."

Procedure:

1) Help your students discuss and complete the Personality Type Preferences sheets.

2) After identifying their personality types, write the names of students on the board under each of the types.

3) Create a personality type bulletin board with a caption listing each type.

4) Have students write their names onto eight strips of paper.

5) Have students pin their strips of paper under each of the eight personality type preferences that most represent them.

6) Hold a discussion with your students about the types of careers each type might prefer; careers in which they could excel by simply being themselves and doing the things that they most prefer doing.

7) Place like types together in cooperative groups for a week and have a classroom discussion at the end of the week about their experiences working together.

8) Change the groups around the following week and attempt to have each type equally represented in a group. Hold another discussion and see how they liked working together.

9) Allow them a week to select their own group and see how equally distributed the personality types are.

Note: Throughout the school year notice how your students are relating to and interacting with each other. Are they truly the type they think they are? What seems to be their best learning situations? What seems to be the best instructional methods for them? Think of ways that you can help them build dreams and identify long-term outcomes that might be suited to their personality types; perhaps careers or things to do that they might not otherwise consider. Be careful not to replace their dreams with your own. Simply expose them to more possibilities.

Name: _____

Instructions: Read the left side and then read the right side and circle the one which *most* applies to you.

A. Extravert*   B. Introvert

I prefer variety, action, and working with others.	I prefer quiet, uninterrupted time for focusing and concentrating. I like to work by myself.
I prefer working on things that I can do quickly so that I can move on to other things.	I like to get really involved in the things that I work on regardless of how long it takes or complicated it is.
It's easy for me to meet, get to know, talk with other people and remember their names.	I don't usually just walk up to someone and start talking. Sometimes I have trouble remembering peoples' names.
I don't like working on things for a long time by myself.	I like working on things until I'm done. I don't mind working by myself.
I'm more interested in getting it done and in seeing how other people do it.	I'm more interested in why we're doing something. What's going to change after it's done?
I like talking to people even when there's nothing much to talk about.	I don't mind talking to people if there is something important to talk about, but I don't like to talk just to be talking.
I don't mind being interrupted when I'm working on something.	I don't like being interrupted when I'm working on something.
I prefer to work quickly, sometimes before giving a lot of thought about what I'm going to do.	I like to think about what I'm going to do before I start working.
I prefer to work with and be around other people.	I prefer working alone or with people who don't talk while working.
It's easy for me to share my thoughts, ideas, and opinions with other people.	Sometimes it's difficult for me to communicate what's on my mind to other people.
I talk a lot.	I don't usually talk a lot.

*Extrovert in some literature

Adapted from Isabel Briggs Myers/Peter B. Myers, *Gifts Differing*.

Wynn/Blassie • © 1995 Rising Sun Publishing • (800) 524-2813   – 119 –
Building Dreams: Elementary School Edition Teacher's Guide

Name: _____

Instructions: Read the left side and then read the right side and circle the one which *most* applies to you.

A. Sensitive

B. Intuitive

I don't like new problems and surprises unless I already know what to do or how to solve the problem.

I like it when we have regular assignments that are done the same way each time.

I feel good about the things that I already know. I don't want to waste time learning a bunch of new stuff.

I like to have an idea of how long it's going to take me to complete an assignment.

I like to take my time and work on things step by step.

I want to talk about exactly what needs to be done.

I don't like working on complicated things.

I don't get that excited about doing something new.

I think more about how things are.

I like solving new problems.

I don't like doing the same thing or working on the same thing over and over. I want to look at how to do it better.

I want to learn whatever I need to know to do what I want to do. I don't care how many new things I have to learn to achieve my goal.

I don't mind working on a project as long as it takes. I'm excited about doing things regardless of how long I have to work on it.

I can make up my mind quickly and work on everything at once to achieve my goal.

I don't like wasting time talking about what we're going to do I just want to get started and do it.

I don't mind things being complicated as long as I know what's suppose to be done.

I get excited about doing new things.

I think more about how things could be.

Adapted from Isabel Briggs Myers/Peter B. Myers, Gifts Differing.

Name: _____

Instructions: Read the left side and then read the right side and circle the one which *most* applies to you.

A. Thinking

I don't usually show my feelings and I prefer dealing with facts more than dealing with people's feelings.

Sometimes I hurt other people and their feelings without knowing it.

I like figuring things out and putting things in order.

I don't mind if other people don't agree with me.

I think more about how "I" think things should be done and what makes sense to "me."

It's more important for me to be treated fairly.

I don't mind being in charge and giving other people responsibilities.

I would rather know what people think.

I tend to think things through and then make up my mind.

I think that we should always follow the class procedures. No excuses.

B. Feeling

It's easy for me to share with people how I feel and I'm usually aware of other people and their feelings.

I go out of my way not to hurt other people's feelings and I try to make other people happy.

I like for things to work smoothly even if everything is not in order.

I like for everyone to agree and get along. I don't like to see people upset.

I like to consider how other people feel about what I'm doing. I'm willing to change if it makes other people happy.

It's more important for people to tell me that I'm doing a good job.

I don't want to hurt people's feelings by making them do things that they don't want to do.

I would rather know how people feel.

I would rather listen to how other people feel and change my mind if necessary to make them happy.

I think that we should listen to why someone violated class procedures and before we decide consider their excuses.

Adapted from Isabel Briggs Myers/Peter B. Myers, *Gifts Differing*.

Name: _____

Instructions: Read the left side and then read the right side and circle the one which *most* applies to you.

A. Judging

B. Perceiving

I work best when I can plan my work and follow the plan.

I don't mind changes once I have begun my work even if it means doing things in a way other than I had planned.

I like to get things completed and finished.

I don't mind leaving things incomplete and open for changes.

It doesn't take me long to make up my mind about something.

I sometimes have trouble making up my mind.

I don't like to interrupt what I'm working on to start a new project.

I sometimes start a lot of projects at the same time and have difficulty finishing them.

I sometimes don't notice, or forget some of the new things that need to be done.

I sometimes put off things that I don't want to do even though I know that it will have to get done.

I just need to know the important things necessary so that I can get started.

I want to know all about the assignment. What are we suppose to do? When do you want it turned in? Why are we doing this?

Once I learn what I need to know I want to go onto something else.

My mind is never totally made up. I'm always interested in learning more about something and in other ways of doing it.

Adapted from Isabel Briggs Myers/Peter B. Myers, *Gifts Differing*.

Personality Types Tally

Extravert*   Introvert

_____   _____

Sensitive   Intuitive

_____   _____

Feeling   Thinking

_____   _____

Judging   Perceiving

_____   _____

*Extrovert in some literature

Activity 24

Learning Styles

Objectives

- To help students identify their unique learning styles and gain an appreciation of the unique learning styles represented in their classroom.

- To gather background information that will help in establishing cooperative groups and in structuring activities.

Materials

- Learning Style sheets.

"Each of us has a special and unique learning style. Like our personality type our learning style reflects the situations, environment, and ways in which we best learn. To help us help each other to become successful, we should know as much about how we like to learn as possible so that we can accommodate, as best we can, everyone in our class."

"For example, raise your hand if you prefer to read while sitting on the floor? What about in a regular school chair? What about on a pillow or bean bag?"

"Well, we're going to learn a little more about ourselves and how we like to learn."

Tracie Barrett is a teacher who not only recognizes the diversity of learning styles, personality types, and culture of her students but who also recognizes the need to fan students on a hot day!

Procedure:

1) As in the personality types activity, help your students discuss and complete the Learning Styles sheets.

2) Help students to identify the ways in which they prefer to learn and write the names of students on the board under the two styles.

3) Add the learning styles captions to your personality types bulletin board.

4) Have each student write his/her name onto a strip of paper.

5) Have each student pin their strip of paper under one of the two learning style preferences.

6) Look at the learning styles. Are they equally divided?

7) Hold a discussion with your students about how we can best help each other to become successful and accommodate both learning styles in our classroom.

8) Identify how each of the learning styles are represented in each of the personality type groupings.

9) Divide the class into each of the learning style groupings for a week and adjust the environment as best as possible to accommodate each group, e.g., soft lighting, snacks, soft furniture, reading stories, listening to stories, etc.

10) At the end of the week, discuss how the students felt about being grouped together. Did any students change groups?

Note: Evaluate and note any effects on individual behavior by working in the new classroom conditions. What about learning, comprehension, remaining on task, etc.? Note how you can best accommodate both types of learners.

Allow people who already have a passionate interest in the arts, sciences, entrepreneurship, sports, music, dancing, civic affairs, etc., to develop and facilitate extracurricular activities and experiences to introduce our students to.

Help students to structure special interest groups or clubs, e.g., young writer's club, young medical club, young entrepreneur's club, young law club, future teacher's of America, and the professional speakers club.

Academic skill development is tied to the particular areas of interests that stimulate their emotional and creative development.

— Mychal Wynn, *Building Dreams: Helping Students Discover Their Potential*

Name: _____

Instructions: Read the left side and then read the right side and circle the one which *most* applies to you.

A. **I like to analyze**	**B.** **I like to globalize**
I prefer things to be quiet so that I can concentrate while I learn.	I prefer noise like music, talking, or TV in the background while I learn.
I prefer to work in groups where we talk <u>after</u> we finish working.	I prefer to work in groups where we talk <u>while</u> we work.
I prefer to talk <u>after</u> I eat.	I prefer to talk <u>while</u> I eat.
I prefer bright lights while I learn.	I prefer soft lighting while I learn.
I prefer sitting at a table, desk or chair while I learn.	I prefer informal and relaxing seating like a bean bag, pillow, rocking chair, bed, carpet, or lying on the floor while I learn.
I prefer working on one thing at a time until I complete it then I'm ready to work on something else.	I prefer working on several things at a time with "breaks" like snacks, or going to the bathroom in between.
I prefer snacking (eating, drinking, or chewing gum) <u>after</u> I have completed my work.	I prefer to snack, eat, drink, or chew gum <u>while</u> I do my work.
I prefer to take notes while the teacher is talking.	I can remember most of what the teacher says without taking notes.
I learn best when I write things down and when the teacher gives me written instructions.	I learn best when the teacher tells me what to do.
I prefer teachers who walk around while they talk.	I prefer teachers who sit at their desks or stand in front of the board when they talk.
I prefer to read a story.	I prefer the teacher to tell a story.
I learn best by watching.	I learn best by listening.
I prefer working alone.	I prefer working in groups.

Wynn/Blassie • © 1995 Rising Sun Publishing • (800) 524-2813

Building Dreams: Elementary School Edition Teacher's Guide

Adapted from Dunn, Dunn, and Treffinger, Bringing Out The Giftedness In Your Child.

Learning Styles Tally

Those who like to analyze

_____

Those who like to globalize

_____

> Most children learn in one of two different processing styles—analytic or global.
>
> Analytic learners learn most easily when information is introduced to them step-by-step or fact-by-fact. Analytics do not mind concentrating on what seem to be unrelated facts as long as they feel they are moving toward a gradual understanding.
>
> Global learners would find the analytic approach incredibly boring. Instead, globals learn best through short stories. When globals hear a story, they pay attention, particularly if the story is about something they recognize or something that interests them. Globals also learn through humor, illustrations, symbols, and graphics. They understand things better when they are introduced to them through an anecdote that explains what they need to learn and why they need to learn it. Once globals understand what they need to learn and why, they can concentrate on the details.
>
> — Dunn, Dunn, and Treffinger, _Bringing Out The Giftedness In Your Child_

Activity 25

Ways That I'm Smart

Objectives

- To help students identify and understand their unique areas of intelligence.

- To help students appreciate the unique ways in which they learn and the special gifts and talents that they've developed.

Materials

- Multiple Intelligences activity sheets.

"There is a professor at Harvard University in Boston, Massachusetts, named Dr. Howard Gardner who has discovered that each of us has at least seven ways in which we learn. We also know that people express themselves differently in each of the seven ways. Over time, some people become so good at expressing themselves in one or more of these ways that we say that they've developed a special gift."

"I'll bet that each of you can recognize someone, including yourself, who is good in one or more of these seven areas. For example: raise your hand if you're good at sports. What about drawing? What about singing or playing a musical instrument? What about talking? What about reading? What about dancing? What about math?"

"Let's look at each of the seven areas and identify the ones we're good at."

Test scores tell us about only a limited number of areas of human performance. By some estimates, a typical IQ test measures only 10 or 15 percent of the many abilities that have been identified and can be described with some degree of accuracy.

IQ tests are a good measure of short-term memory, vocabulary, and spatial reasoning.

But the tests miss *creative imagination, leadership, social sensibility, interpersonal ability, artistic* or *musical ability, mechanical aptitude,* and *practical abilities* ("street smarts").

Understanding giftedness in terms of an IQ score means overlooking or disregarding a number of talents that most of us would think of as gifts.

— Dunn, Dunn, and Treffinger, *Bringing Out The Giftedness In Your Child*

Procedure:

1) Create a caption and call it "Our Multiple Intelligences."

2) List each of the intelligences identified by Gardner under the caption.

3) Explain the different areas of intelligence and ask students to identify at least one that they feel that they are good at.

4) Write the names of students under each of the areas that they believe that they are good at.

5) Explore the types of careers where people benefit from the areas of intelligence that the students have identified.

6) Explore the relationships between the areas of intelligences identified by students and the personality type board.

7) Create visuals (e.g., clouds, bricks, hands, etc.) and write the possible career aspirations representative of the intelligences represented in your classroom. Cover the complete spectrum from auto mechanic to President. Post these around the room or suspend them from the ceiling.

8) Ask your students to identify how combined intelligences can enhance career aspirations.

Example:

Verbal/Linguistic—Logical/Mathematical could combine to create a fun-loving, joke-telling, Math teacher.

Intrapersonal—Musical/Rhythmic could combine to create a sensitive song writing singer or musician.

9) Ask your students to continue this activity and write down possible career aspirations for their combined intelligences.

10) Post the intelligences under your "Multiple Intelligences" caption.

11) Post your students' names beneath each of the areas that they've identified that they're strongest in.

Name: _____

Instructions: Read the list and check the box for those areas that you are good at.

☐ **Verbal/Linguistic:**

I'm good at things like reading, writing, talking, and debating.

I like things like poetry, humor, storytelling, debating, and creative writing.

☐ **Logical/Mathematical:**

I'm good at figuring things out, analyzing things, and solving problems in subjects like math and science.

I like things like figuring out patterns, matching things that are alike, math, science, crossword puzzles, and solving problems.

☐ **Intrapersonal:**

I'm good at understanding other people's feelings. I'm also good at focusing and concentrating, and thinking things through.

I like things like closing my eyes and reflecting about how I feel about things, focusing, concentrating, and understanding how other people feel. I like meditating and thinking about things.

☐ **Interpersonal:**

I'm good at working with other people and working on group projects. I'm also good at sharing my opinion with other people, understanding their opinions and how they feel about things.

I like to work with other people on group projects and in sharing ideas and opinions.

Building Dreams: Elementary School Edition © 1995 RISING SUN PUBLISHING (800) 524-2813

Name: _____

Instructions: Read the list and check the box for those areas that you are good at.

☐ **Visual/Spatial:**

I'm good at creating pictures in my mind and drawing them. I'm also good at creative, artistic things, using colors, reading maps, and I have a good imagination.

I like to draw, paint, create sculptures, and imagine things.

☐ **Body/Kinesthetic:**

I'm good at things like sports, dance, gymnastics, karate, and boxing. I'm also good at working with my hands. I have good body control and coordination.

I like things like playing sports, dancing, exercising, swimming, skating, riding bicycles, running, and building things.

☐ **Musical/Rhythmic:**

I'm good at things like picking up sounds and tones, keeping a beat and remembering melodies.

I like singing, playing musical instruments, beating drums, humming, writing songs, and performing.

Review the areas that you are good at and select the ONE area that you believe you're *best* and that you *really* enjoy.

For example: I have a highly developed Logical/Mathematical intelligence and a highly developed Verbal/Linguistic Intelligence. My best and favorite thing to do is to write so I would select Verbal/Linguistic Intelligence as my one choice.

Indicate your choice: _____

Building Dreams: Elementary School Edition © 1995 RISING SUN PUBLISHING (800) 524-2813

Seven Ways To Discover Your Dreams

Intrapersonal Intelligence
Knowledge of the internal aspects of self such as: feelings, range of emotional responses, self-reflection, and sense of intuition about spiritual realities.

Visual/Spatial Intelligence
Ability to create internal mental pictures. Deals with such things as the visual arts, navigation, map-making, and architecture.

Logical/Mathematical Intelligence
Associated with what we call "scientific thinking." Deductive/inductive thinking/reasoning, numbers and recognition of abstract patterns.

Verbal/Linguistic Intelligence
Responsible for the production of language and all the complex possibilities that follow, including: poetry, humor, storytelling, abstract reasoning, and the written word.

Musical/Rhythmic Intelligence
Includes such capacities as the recognition and use of rhythmic and tonal patterns, sensitivity to sounds such as the human voice and musical instruments.

Interpersonal Intelligence
Ability to work cooperatively in a group as well as the ability to communicate, verbally and non-verbally with other people.

Body/Kinesthetic Intelligence
Ability to use the body to express emotion as in dance, body language, and sports. The ability to learn by doing.

Building Dreams: Elementary School Edition © 1995 RISING SUN PUBLISHING (800) 524-2813

Howard Gardner has identified seven intelligences—seven distinct ways that we learn and know about reality—and believes there may be more. [Seven Ways of Knowing: Teaching for Multiple Intelligences. David Lazear]

Seven Styles of Learning

Type	Likes To	Is Good At	Learns Best By
Verbal/Linguistic *"The Word Player"*	read, write, tell stories	memorizing names, places, dates, trivia	saying, hearing, and seeing words
Logical/Mathematical *"The Questioner"*	do experiments, figure things out, work with numbers, ask questions	math reasoning, logic, problem solving	categorizing, classifying, working with abstract patterns/relationships
Visual/Spatial *"The Visualizer"*	draw, build, design and create things, daydream, look at pictures, watch movies	imagining things, sensing changes, mazes/puzzles, reading maps, charts	visualizing, dreaming, using the mind's eye, working with colors and pictures
Musical/Rhythmic *"The Music Lover"*	sing, hum tunes, listen to music, play an instrument, respond to music	picking up sounds, remembering melodies, keeping time	rhythm, melody, music
Bodily/Kinesthetic *"The Mover"*	move around, touch and talk, use body language	physical activities, sports, dance, acting, crafts	touching, moving, interacting with space, processing knowledge through bodily sensations
Interpersonal *"The Socializer"*	have lots of friends, talk to people, join groups	understanding people, leading others, organizing, communicating, manipulating, mediating conflicts	sharing, comparing, relating, cooperating, interviewing
Intrapersonal *"The Individual"*	work alone, pursue own interests	understanding self, focusing inward on feelings, dreams, following instincts, pursuing interests, goals, being original	working alone, individualized projects, self-paced instruction, having own space

© 1995 Rising Sun Publishing (800) 524-2813

Wynn/Blassie • © 1995 Rising Sun Publishing • (800) 524-2813
Building Dreams: Elementary School Edition Teacher's Guide

Activity 26

Who I Am

Objectives

- To help students gain appreciation for the uniqueness of their homes, families, and culture.

Materials

- Who I Am activity sheets.

"I would like for each of you to take the sheet of paper that I am going to hand out and complete it for what you do after school today and what you do before school tomorrow."

"We are going to post the sheets onto a bulletin board called 'Who We Are.' We are going to select a different sheet each day and read it and see if we can guess who is being described."

Billy loved to invent crazy machines. One of them caused water to run down a chute, moving ping-pong balls into sockets, causing bells to ring and a miniature pig to spin around. This finally moved an alligator's head into which you could stick your pencil to be sharpened. Other machines did similarly creative and practical things. Yet in spite of these innovative projects, Billy was flunking out of school. He couldn't seem to do things the school's way. For example, when Billy's mother asked him to figure out the area of a room using the methods the school had taught him, Billy struggled. He tensed his body, erased frequently, and finally came up with a totally unrealistic answer.

Then Billy did it his way. "Billy shut his eyes and made little rhythmic movements with his head, as if he were listening to an inner song. After a while he jotted down something on the pad, closed his eyes for some more internal business, opened them, jotted something else down, and gave us the correct answer." Asked to describe the process, Billy responded, "Well, when I close my eyes to figure something out it's like a cross between music and architecture."

— Thomas Armstrong, *In Their Own Way*

Who I Am

I was born in _____

My birthday is _____

In addition to English I speak _____

Describe your family:

_____

_____

_____

Describe where you live:

_____

_____

_____

Describe your brothers, sisters, and pets:

_____

_____

My favorite things to do are:

_____

_____

My favorite places to go are:

_____

_____

My favorite things to eat are:

_____

_____

A School Day in The Life of Mychal-David Wynn (first grade)

I wake up at 6:30 in the morning. Sometimes I wake up by myself and sometimes my mom comes into my room and wakes me up. Sometimes my dad comes in and wakes me up.

The first thing that I do is eat breakfast. My mom usually fixes me oatmeal, cream of wheat or cereal. My favorite cereal is Fruit Loops. Sometimes my dad makes my breakfast. He usually makes scrambled eggs with cheese. My dad knows that's my favorite breakfast.

My mom feeds my baby brother, Jalani, while I eat my breakfast.

After breakfast I brush my teeth, wash my face, and put on my clothes. My mom lays my clothes out for me.

After I put my clothes on, my mom brushes my hair. I get my Back Pack and get ready to go to the bus stop. I have to open the blinds in the living room before I go to the bus stop.

My dad walks me to the bus stop. Sometimes we play catch before the bus comes. Sometimes we race remote control cars and sometimes we just race to the bus stop. My dad lets me win.

I'm the first stop for the bus driver so I have a choice of any seat. I usually sit in the second row. The bus ride to school is not very long. When I get off of the bus, sometimes I go to the library before class to return books.

After school I ride the bus home. When I get home, I have a snack. My favorite snack is chocolate chip cookies. After my snack, I do any schoolwork that I have. If I finish in time, I watch TV or play video games until it is time to go to my karate class.

In karate class we practice forms which involve a lot of kicking, blocking, and punching.

After karate class, my mom or dad picks me up and I go home and eat dinner. After dinner, I take a bath. After my bath, I brush my teeth and read a book before I go to bed.

I go to bed at 8:30.

That's a typical school day in my life!

Ways of preparing Students for Success

There are a number of classroom bulletin boards and activities that will help students to identify and focus on positive behavior. The following activities are all designed to help students focus on behavior that is complimentary to others, that positively resolves conflicts, and that provides rewards that everyone can share in as a result of a positive village [classroom] community.

Henry F. Beechhold, in *The Creative Classroom*, notes:

> The classroom is more than anything else a state of mind. . . If, by virtue of the activities which go on and the attitudes which are expressed in the classroom, the student feels that this is the right place for him to be, then we have a classroom worthy of the name, a place for education. But all the carpeting, closed-circuit television, overhead projectors, felt boards, pastel-colored furniture, self-regulating light controls, and restful green chalkboards in the world will make no difference in an atmosphere of compulsion, rigidity, "discipline," and mindless busywork.

We seldom have success forcing students to do anything. However, if we can help them to become self-governing, whereas they work individually toward self respect, respect for others, and are responsible for their actions, they will more readily take ownership of our classroom and over their own behavior. When they fall short of the desired behavior represented by our classroom expectations, they have others within the classroom community to help them. This sense of working together can be achieved no matter which students you're working with, where they come from, what their previous behavior has been, or where they are academically.

Last year we begin talking to our students about their dreams and aspirations. We engaged them in some activities that crystallized for our students "why" they had certain dreams and we demonstrated through our support, encouragement, and classroom discussions what our teaching staff would do to help our students achieve their dreams.

This year we experienced the best first week of school in my four years at Welborn. The students returned to school picking up just where we left off last year. Our teachers engaged students in illustrating their dreams for the early grade levels, and in writing narratives about their dreams for the upper grade levels. We displayed their work and have banners throughout the school encouraging everyone in our school to have a dream.

— Dr. Judi Farmer, Welborn Elementary School, Kansas City, Kansas

Activity 28

Responsible Choices

Objectives

- To help students to become self directed in their behavior.
- To help students internalize how current decisions affect their future potential to achieve their dreams and aspirations.

Materials

- Construction paper.
- Scissors.
- Markers.
- Border.

"We are going to focus our attention on the responsible choices that we should make so that we can live the healthiest, most fulfilling, most satisfying, and most personally rewarding lives that we can."

"Making responsible choices is directly tied to what we learn. For example: babies often hurt themselves by touching fire, or sticking their fingers into electrical sockets, or falling down stairs because they haven't learned how to make responsible choices."

"What are some of the responsible choices that you have learned to make?"

Procedure:

1) "Let's write down some of the responsible choices that you have learned to make on the board."

Example:

Don't do drugs.

Don't drink alcohol.

Learn to read and think for yourself.

Eat healthy foods.

Don't join gangs.

Display positive character values.

2) "Okay, I'm going to write our choices onto the notes that I've prepared for our 'Responsible Choices Bulletin Board' (e.g., clouds, stars, food items, apples, etc.)."

3) "Whenever you learn or think of a responsible choice, write it down on a sheet of paper and I will place it on our 'Responsible Choices Bulletin Board.'"

4) Go over the responsible choices as an example when your students have to make responsible choices.

Sample dialogue:

"John, Mark said something to you that you didn't like and you yelled at Mark. Was yelling at Mark a responsible choice? What are some of the responsible choices that you could have made?"

"Is falling asleep in class a responsible choice? What are some of the responsible choices that you can make if you feel ill or tired?"

5) Go over the responsible choices periodically in class and discuss why they are responsible choices so that your students internalize them.

Activity 29

Traffic Light Book

Objectives

- To help students to become self directed in their behavior.
- To provide students and parents with a visual record of student behavior.

Materials

- Construction paper.
- Scissors.
- Markers.

This activity was developed by an extraordinary teacher, Toni Douglas, my son's pre-kindergarten teacher at Wood Acres Country Day School, in Marietta, Georgia.

"Class, each day before we leave the classroom I am going to give you either a red, yellow, or green sticker to place onto your calendar for that day. These stickers will indicate for your parents what type of behavior you've had that day. Can anyone tell me what type of behavior they think would warrant a green light? Yellow light? Red light?"

With your students, create a traffic light chart that outlines what behavior is associated with each light.

My son brought his Traffic Light Book home each day and proudly exclaimed, "I got a green light today. I have all green lights. Chad didn't get a green light. Chad got a red light because he hit someone on the playground. Chad's not really bad, he was just having a bad day." Each day during the ride from school, my son told me about the school day, always mentioning classroom behavior.

The Traffic Light Book helped my son and many other children, particularly visual learners, focus on their daily behavior and the manner in which they were treating others and resolving conflicts. It was beneficial to parents since it immediately brought their attention to challenging days. Many of the children could look back over a month of green lights and if there was a red or yellow light, they could recall the particular challenge that they had on that day.

Procedure:

1) Take two 8 1/2 by 11 sheets of green construction paper.

2) Write "My Traffic Light Book" across the top.

3) Beneath the words, draw or paste a large traffic light colored with red, yellow, and green lights.

4) Laminate the sheets of construction paper so that they can withstand the wear and tear of the school year.

5) Inside the book, place a copy of a monthly calendar for each month of the school year.

6) Staple the sheets of construction paper, together with the enclosed calendar sheets, to create a book.

7) Give a book to each student and explain the behaviors associated with each light.

My Traffic Light Book

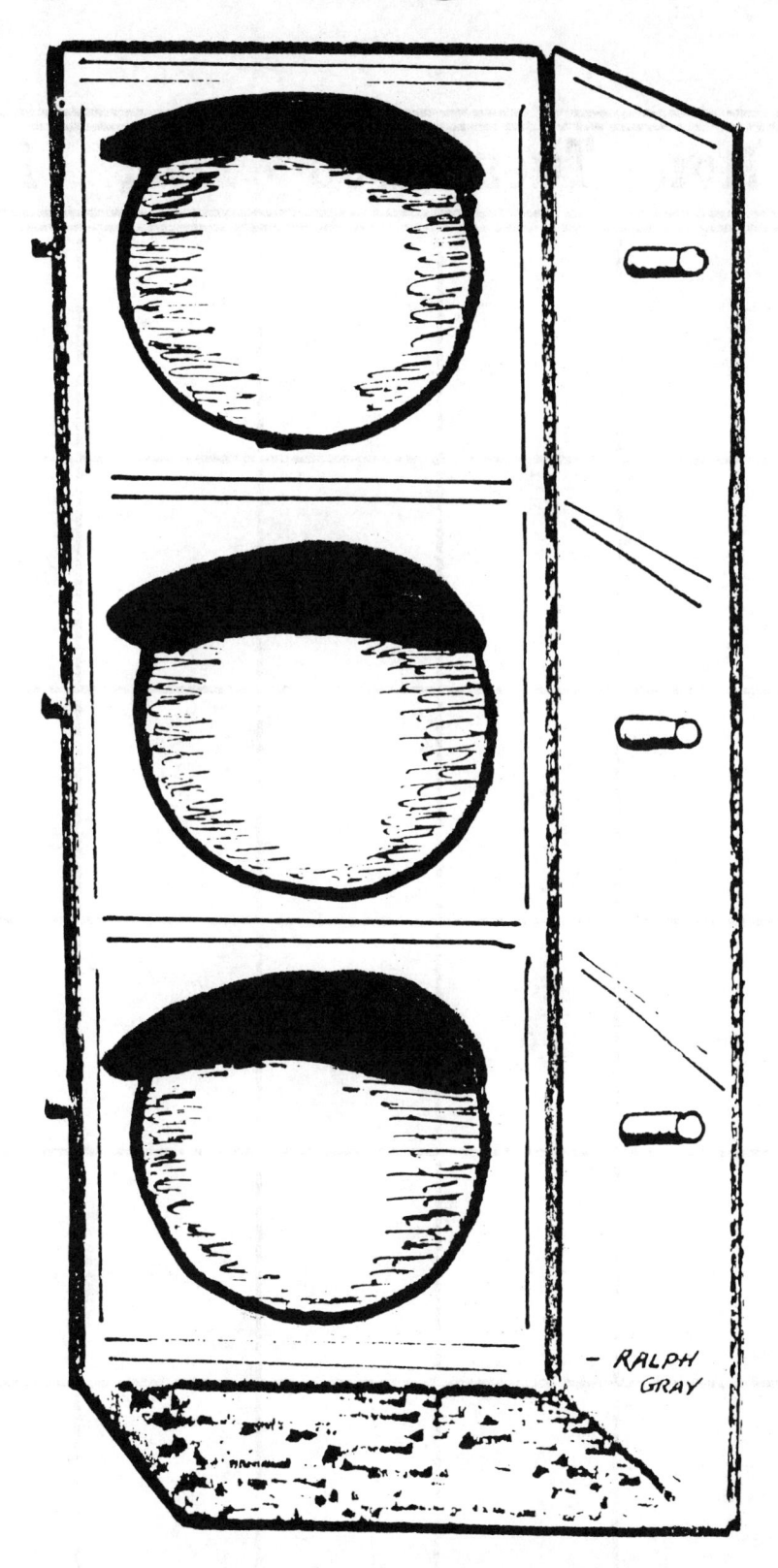

— RALPH GRAY

Sun	Mon	Tues	Wed	Thur	Fri	Sat

Activity 30

Habits

Objectives

- To help students to become self directed in their behavior.

- To help students understand how good habits can contribute toward healthy choices while bad habits can hinder them.

- To help students increase comprehension skills through objective self assessment.

Materials

- Construction paper.
- Scissors.
- Markers.
- Border.

"We are going to discuss habits. Can someone explain to the class what a *habit* is?"

"A habit is something that a person does repetitively and often without even thinking about it like picking your nose, cracking your knuckles, chewing on your finger nails, or tapping your fingers on the desk. A habit can also be an addiction like cigarette smoking, alcohol, or drugs. Can someone give me an example of a habit?"

"What do you think is the difference between a good habit and a bad habit?"

Habit: A recurrent, often unconscious pattern of behavior that is acquired through frequent repetition. An addiction, especially to a narcotic drug.

Procedure:

1) Have students take a sheet of paper and write down the definition of a habit.

2) Have students list good habits that they have.

"List all of the things that you do regularly that you would consider good habits. Do you read books everyday? Do you eat healthy foods everyday? Do you exercise everyday? Do you say something nice or positive about someone everyday? Do you complete all of your classroom assignments by the day that they're due?"

3) Have students list bad habits that they have.

"List all of the things that you do regularly that you would consider bad habits. For example, someone might consider their bad habits to be things like; I don't read books unless I'm forced to; I eat a lot of candy; I watch a lot of TV; I never exercise unless the PE teacher makes me; I turn in my work late; I forget my assignments; I put people down; I disobey my parents; I forget my responsibilities at home."

4) Engage students in a classroom discussion about some bad habits and what a person could do to replace their bad habits with good habits.

"Lets discuss some bad habits that you wrote down and identify at least three good habits that could replace them. For example, if someone had a bad habit of turning their assignments in late the good habits that they could replace the bad habit with could be:

A) Starting to work on assignments immediately and not putting them off.

B) Get a study partner who could help them focus on when the assignment is due.

C) Always have assignments ready at least a day before they are due."

5) Have each student complete the Bad Habits/Good Habits sheet on the following page.

6) Create a Habit bulletin board or a Falling into Good Habits Tree. On one side, place the heading Bad Habits and on the other, Good Habits.

7) Post each student's habits onto the Habit Bulletin Board or Good Habits Tree.

"It takes a lot of hard work to overcome bad habits. The only way to overcome a bad habit is to replace it with a good habit. That's why it's always good to develop good habits as early as possible to help keep bad habits from ever developing. As each one of you replaces your bad habits with a good habit, take your sheet and draw a red circle with an X through it over your bad habit and post your sheet onto the good habit side. This means that you have worked hard to overcome your bad habit and that you are well on your way to achieving your dreams and aspirations."

8) "Each time that you overcome a bad habit, look on your list and select another bad habit that you want to work on. Write down three good habits that you want to replace it with and post it under the bad habits category."

Have a celebration each week of all of the bad habits that your students have overcome.

Dreaming Eagles

Once there was a marvelous elementary school with courteous, wonderful students. The school was staffed by a loyal, kind, confident, compassionate, and outstanding staff. It was the dream of each teacher to develop and encourage each student to meet the challenges of every day life with determination and fortitude.

The students were taught to face life with dignity and integrity that would lead to strong self esteem and self respect. They were courteous, helpful, loyal, and kind to their fellow students and teachers.

The school is Felton Laboratory School, staffed with a group of Eagles as teachers, whose goal in life is to tap the creative genius in each student, and help these young eagles soar to insurmountable heights.

— Felton Laboratory School, Orangeburg, South Carolina

Student: _____

To achieve my dreams and aspirations, I should replace my bad habits with good habits.

I believe that some of my bad habits are:

_____
_____
_____
_____

Good Habits that I can replace my Bad Habits with:

_____
_____
_____
_____
_____
_____
_____
_____

Building Dreams: Elementary School Edition © 1995 RISING SUN PUBLISHING (800) 524-2813

Activity 31

Burying "I CAN'T"

Objectives

- To help students to eliminate negative thinking.
- To help students focus on more positive and constructive ways of phrasing a problem.
- To help raise student self esteem and self image.

Materials

- Construction paper.
- Shoe box or other small box.

"Class, one of the worst habits that a person can develop is negative thinking. You can tell when a person has developed this habit because you will here them constantly talking about what they can't do, what they can't achieve, what they can't learn, and so forth."

"So we are going to bury 'I Can't' forever. Because we cannot help each other to become successful as long as we are focusing our attention on what we believe that we cannot do, we have to focus our attention on how to do what we don't currently know how to do. For example, there was a time when none of you could read, walk, or feed yourselves. Just think of where you would be if someone had taught you to say, 'I Can't' and made you believe that you couldn't before you learned how to do these things!"

Procedure:

1) Have your students take out a sheet of paper and list all of the things that they may say or think that they can't do. [An alternative is that you list things on the board.]

2) Walk around the class and remind students about things that you've heard them say in the past that they couldn't do.

3) Think of things for them to add to their lists if they need encouragement.

Example:

"I can't fly an airplane or helicopter; eat at an expensive restaurant; travel to another country; fly first class; sail around the world; read 10 books a day; recite the ABC's backward; get a perfect score on the spelling test; do ten push-ups; eat only one cookie, etc."

4) Have all of the students form a line. Have them stand before the class and one by one select one of the things from their list and affirm "I can learn how to. . ." Give an applause to each student as they affirm what they can learn.

5) Collect their lists and place them into a box representing a coffin and perform a ceremonial burial.

6) Do a collaborative illustration of a tombstone and have everyone in your classroom sign it. List on the tombstone, "I Can't" and the date that you put him to rest.

7) Perform a Eulogy (see the following page).

8) Whenever you hear a student say, "I Can't," point to the tombstone and allow the student to rephrase the statement.

Burying "I CAN'T"

"Friends, we gather today to honor the memory of 'I Can't.' While he was with us on earth, he touched the lives of everyone, some more than others. His name, unfortunately, has been spoken in every public building — schools, city halls, state capitols, and yes, even in The White House."

"We have provided a final resting place for 'I Can't.' 'I Will' and 'I'm Going to Right Away' are not as well known as their famous relative, and are certainly not as strong and powerful yet. Perhaps some day, with your help, they will make an even bigger mark on the world."

"May 'I Can't' rest in peace and may everyone present here pick up their lives and move forward in his absence. Amen."

They celebrated the passing of "I Can't" with cookies, popcorn, and fruit juices. As part of the celebration, Donna cut out a large tombstone from butcher paper. She wrote the words "I Can't" at the top and put RIP in the middle. The date was added at the bottom.

The paper tombstone hug in Donna's classroom for the remainder of the year. On those rare occasions when a student forgot and said, "I Can't," Donna simply pointed to the RIP sign. The student then remembered that "I Can't" was dead and chose to rephrase the statement.

Now, years later, whenever I hear the phrase, "I Can't," I see images of that fourth-grade funeral. Like the students, I remember that "I Can't" is dead.

— Excerpt from Chick Moorman, *Chicken Soup for the Soul*

I'm not old enough to play baseball or football. I'm not eight yet. My mom told me when you start baseball, you aren't going to be able to run that fast because you had an operation. I told Mom I wouldn't need to run that fast. When I play baseball, I'll just hit them out of the park. Then I'll be able to walk.

— Edward J. McGrath, Jr. *An Exceptional View of Life*

Activity 32

Back Pack Book Club

Objectives

- To help students develop the habit of carrying books.
- To motivate students to read more.

Materials

- Book forms.

"Class, we are going to have a club this year called the 'Back Pack Book Club.' Everyone in the class is automatically a member because the Back Pack Book Club is going to prepare you to become successful."

"Each Monday, we are going to wear our Back Pack Book Club badges. Our badges will display how many books we have read during the previous week and how many books we have read this year. We are going to keep a total for each person in our classroom and for the total number of books that our entire classroom has read."

"Reading is perhaps the most important step to preparing us to become successful. It is through reading and comprehension that we are able to learn all of the things that we need to know to become successful."

"We are not in competition with each other. Each person needs to do the best he or she can. Whatever you do will count toward the total number of books read by our classroom."

Procedure:

1) Create a Back Pack Book Club bulletin board. Place book covers, topics, etc., onto the board.

2) Create Back Pack Book Club badges (see sample on following page).

3) Give each student a book chart to keep track of the books read.

4) Help the students create folders to keep their book charts. These folders can become a reference book by year-end of the books they've read.

5) Have students total their books each Monday and note their individual totals on the board. Have the students write their individual weekly totals and cumulative totals on their Back Pack Book Club badges.

6) Total the number of books read by the class. Have students write the total books read by the class on their badges.

7) Create special badges for different categories such as:

    - Most books read this week.
    - Most improved.
    - Most books read this year.

8) Create a bookworm noting title, author, date read, and student's name.

Back Pack Book Club

Date: _____

_____ is a member in good standing in the Back Pack Book Club and is actively reading for success.

Number of books I read last week: _____

Number of books I've read this year: _____

Number of books my class read last week: _____

Total books my class has read this year: _____

© 1995 Rising Sun Publishing (800) 524-2813

The Back Pack Book Club helps to prevent the transformation of students as noted by Alfie Kohn, in *Punished by Rewards*, who comments:

When they first get to school, they are endlessly fascinated by the world. They are filled with delight by their newfound ability to print their own names in huge, shaky letters, to count everything in sight, to decode the signs they see around them. They sit on the floor at story time, eyes wide and jaws slack, listening raptly as the teacher reads. They come home bubbling with new facts and new connections between facts. "You know what we learned today?"

By the time the last bell has rung, the spell has been broken. Their eyes have narrowed. They complain about homework. They count the minutes until the end of the period, the days left before the weekend, the weeks they must endure until the next vacation. "Do we have to know this?"

. . . students may be left not only regarding learning as a chore but regarding themselves as unequal to the task. In any case, there is nothing natural about these changes. . . If children's' enthusiasm is smothered, it is a direct result of something that happens in our schools. No single factor can completely account for this dismaying transformation.

Date	Title of Book	Read to child	Read with child	Read by child	Parent Signature
	1				
	2				
	3				
	4				
	5				
	6				
	7				
	8				
	9				
	10				
	11				
	12				
	13				
	14				
	15				
	16				
	17				
	18				

Outside Mrs. Woodham's 2nd grade classroom students see literacy as the road along which "We are making responsible choices to achieve our dreams!"

Mrs. Woodham's 2nd grade students set a goal to extend their bookworm completely around the school. They know that you must read to succeed!

Wynn/Blassie • © 1995 Rising Sun Publishing • (800) 524-2813
Building Dreams: Elementary School Edition Teacher's Guide

Dream-Building Activities

What we have done so far is prepare our students to become successful by creating a warm, welcoming, risk-free environment. The Dream Classroom is full of colors, images, words, phrases, ideas, and opportunities that stimulate the senses and help students to look forward to the potential and possibilities of life.

No dream is too large or too small. The recurring questions in a Dream Classroom are, "What do you have to do to achieve your dreams? What knowledge do you need? What work must you do? What preparations must you make? What experiences or skills must you gain? What type of character must you develop? What support will you need? What value will achieving your dreams have on your family, community, and in the world around you?

Dream-building activities provide insight into what information and additional resources are needed. Work together with your students, their families, colleagues, mentors, your school's alumni association and any person or agency that will have you to help your students achieve their dreams.

Prepare your students for success!

In my classroom, we've contacted Parkway's Alumni Association which has helped us find guest speakers from motivational speakers to doctors. We even had a Horseman come with a horse. He showed our students how to take care of a horse, how to put a saddle on, how to mount, and how to ride. This resulted from the dreams of a student to become a competitive horseback rider.

We had a professional singer who came to our classroom and demonstrated to our students how to sing, how to get started in the singing profession, what to do, who to know, etc., because one of our students had dreams and aspirations of becoming a professional singer.

We've had models, actresses, artists, archaeologists, electricians, gymnasts, and many others representing the dreams and aspirations of our students. Our students don't believe that they have to wait. They believe in making their dreams a reality today by focusing their vision and working toward their dreams daily.

Mychal Wynn visited our classroom near the end of the school year. Parents watched as Mr. Wynn spoke to the students about their dreams and aspirations. I held my breath as Mr. Wynn asked my students "How has Mrs. Blassie helped you this year to achieve your dreams?"

I was bubbling with pride as my students, one by one, articulated what their dreams were and how we had worked together throughout the school to prepare them for success. They articulated the various activities that we had engaged in, the guest speakers whom they had heard, and how we had all been working together.

Mr. Wynn then asked the students, "Raise your hand if every teacher that you've had has asked you what your dreams and aspirations were?" Sadly, not one of my students raised a hand. Mr. Wynn then asked, "Raise your hand if most of your teachers have asked you what your dreams and aspirations were?" Again, not a single student raised their hand. Finally, Mr. Wynn asked, "Raise your hand if just one teacher, other than Mrs. Blassie, has ever asked you what your dreams and aspirations were?" Only three students raised their hands.

Mr. Wynn went on to talk to the students about how they could become dream weavers in their classes the coming year. One student particularly, Jeremiah, said that he would like to talk to other teachers to tell them what the Dream Classroom is about, that if they could make their classrooms Dream Classrooms, then more children would want to come to school!

By joining with parents, we are helping children to become "dream specific." Identification of and directions toward one's personal pursuits is happening through combined parental and student involvement. Through resources and research, my students are experiencing examples of sought-after dreams like spending time with a horse to become a horseman someday, or visiting a professional singer, actor, or pianist to become a professional like them some day.

Perhaps the best dream weaver of all who visited our class was the veterinarian who brought x-rays and animals so that the students could pretend that they were doctors. Several students changed their dreams after that visit. They left class with ambitions of becoming veterinarians and to join the fight for animal rights!

The risk-free environment of a Dream Classroom encourages and allows students to feel secure. Opportunities are endless and the benefits are immediate. Classroom experiences are infused and given greater meaning in our daily learning. Oh, how my students have felt successful!

Amie missed the first three days of school because of personal difficulties. To hide how frightened she must have felt when she came into the class, she acted really tough. She was having a difficult time and was constantly being placed into "time out." I talked to Amie one day during recess and I asked, "Amie what can I do to help you? How can I help you to become successful? Is there anything that I can do or that anyone else can do? Is there anybody whom you would like to sit next to who would make you happy or help you to become successful."

Amie said, "Yeah, that girl over there," as she motioned to another girl named Renee. I motioned Renee over and I asked, "Renee would you like to assist Amie and help her to become successful?" Renee said, "Sure, I don't mind at all. I'll help Amie become successful." When we returned to the classroom, Amie and Renee sat next to each other. Renee helped Amie with her homework and helped her to pay attention in class. I called both parents to tell them about the interaction between Renee and Amie. Renee seemed to feel good about helping Amie and Amie seemed to feel good that someone was eager to assist her.

There was another student, Nikkie, who wanted to become an artist. I asked her if she wanted to start training now and start feeling successful at becoming a professional artist? Every Friday she gave our class a mini lesson on how to draw. Each student received art paper while Nikkie instructed them using the overhead projector.

What do you want to do and how can we help you?

Jeremiah had an interest in electronics and we had a guest speaker who presented a talk on electricity. I was able to arrange with my principal, Mr. Rob Sainz, and the West Middle School principal, Dr. Sam Sciortino, to allow Jeremiah to participate in an afternoon electronics Dream Apprenticeship. Jeremiah will never forget this dream experience!

Percy had a dream to become a gymnast. I arranged for a taxi to pick him up each day after his gymnastics class to take him home. Mrs. Rita White, our school counselor, was so eager that she facilitated getting money donated from our PTO president, Kathy Strong; Rob Sainz, our principal; Ginny Altrogge, our assistant principal; and me and we were able to buy a gymnastics outfit and to pay for the lessons for Percy.

Percy was so excited by this dream experience that one day in class I asked him how it was going and he said, "Oh, Mrs. Blassie, let me show you. Hey, move those desks over there." Before I could say anything, Percy backed up and did three somersaults down the middle of the classroom.

I shared this story with a group of teachers later in the year at a workshop. I saw one of the teachers who attended the workshop during the summer who shared with me, "Dee I saw Percy the other day in summer school and I went up to him and I shared with him that I knew about his dream of becoming a gymnast as a means of bonding with him. Well, as soon as I asked, "Percy I was talking with Mrs. Blassie about you and she shared with me your dream of becoming a gymnast," Percy responded, "Do you mind if I show you the flip that I can do?"

Setting up the dream classroom is so important to implementing character values. It is so easy to provide all of the students with the feeling of being so successful. The students will feel a sense of belonging.

There are so many ways to get the whole school involved. Last year was the first year we were aware of the fifteen values that the board adopted. So we had a committee consisting of reps from primary, intermediate, and the facilitator who attended the training for character education to decide what values we were going to do each month. We made a list of activities, books to read, and ideas of how to incorporate character education into the curriculum. Each morning we had a saying about what value we were working on for the month. The staff and students really liked the morning sayings.

This is our second year since character education was introduced in Parkway. Our efforts this year is how to implement character education into our curriculum. I am going to demonstrate some ways of how easy it is to implement the fifteen values.

The dream classroom started after I met Mychal Wynn and he crystallized for me what I had been doing for over 18 years in the classroom.

Just because you have a college degree in English does not make you a teacher, much less an English teacher. You need to know about academic learning time, formative and summative testing, criterion-referenced testing, discipline plans, procedures and routines, learning styles, motivational theory, record-keeping procedures, identification of learning disabilities, higher-order thinking skills, due process, privacy rights, grouping, community services, mastery learning, remediation and correction, prescriptive learning, credibility, and a whole host of other things.

Having a degree in English is the last thing you need. The first thing you need to know is how to manage a classroom full of students. You were not hired to teach third grade, coach football, or teach English. You were hired to take a group of possibly disinterested, howling, and unruly people and turn them into interested, disciplined, and productive learners in a well-managed environment.

— Harry K. Wong, *The First Days of School*

Activity 33

Classroom Curriculum Goals

Objectives

- To help students understand the process of goal-setting and how attaining small goals leads to attaining larger goals.

- To help students understand your requirements for achieving academic goals for the year.

Materials

- Large poster board or pre-printed posters.

"To achieve our dreams and aspirations, we have to set goals. Goals are the steps that we believe that we must take to turn our dreams into reality. They also represent the various things that we would like to achieve such as smaller dreams that lead to achieving bigger dreams."

"For example, when we study for a test, we all could have a goal of answering each question correctly which implies that we really understand what we've learned. Someone who likes to draw might have a goal of drawing illustrations that would be published in a book. See how goals can represent the steps necessary to achieve our dreams?"

"On our goal chart I am going to list each of the steps necessary to achieve each grade that I am going to give in each of the subjects that we are going to cover. So, if you have a goal of getting an 'A' in English, then you will know each of the smaller goals or steps necessary in order to get an 'A.' This way, you will always know where you are in relationship to your goal."

Procedure:

1) Create a bulletin board and call it "Our Goals."

2) List each of the areas that you will be grading students in throughout the school year.

3) Place the headings week, month, and year's goals across the top.

4) Note the goals for the material that you want to cover for the current week, month, and the entire school year.

5) Beneath each heading place the completed grade sheets that outline the requirements for each grade (see following page).

What one student said about goals:

Believe in goal setting. By believing in goal setting you should try your hardest. When times get hard, keep trying to achieve your dreams. Goals turn into dreams when you try your best regardless of obstacles that may come along the way in achieving your dreams.

— Robin White, an eighth grade student at West Middle School in Kansas City, Kansas

(Top) Mrs. Woodham's 2nd grade students have their goals displayed on clouds that proudly hang from the ceiling in their classroom. (Bottom) Students also display their goals onto their Field of Dreams (e.g., places to go, things to learn, changes in the world, and careers).

Wynn/Blassie • © 1995 Rising Sun Publishing • (800) 524-2813
Building Dreams: Elementary School Edition Teacher's Guide

Activity 34

Personal Goals

Objectives

- To help students understand how their dreams and aspirations can represent goals that they can strive for throughout their lifetime.
- To help students focus on intermediate, mid-term, and long-term goals.

Materials

- Copies of John Goddard's goals.

"How old do you believe a person has to be before they can begin setting goals?. Well, you probably began setting goals before you could speak. The next time you see a baby trying to walk, you're watching a baby set goals. He or she has set a goal to walk and keeps trying and trying until that goal is achieved."

"How many of you have set goals in the past to make a basket, or hit a baseball, or kick a soccer ball into the net, or catch a football, or mold something out of clay, or create a paper airplane?"

"We set goals all the time in all types of ways. However, most of the time we set small goals like getting up on time to catch the school bus to school, or winning a race in PE. However, there was a young boy, who was fifteen years old, who sat down at his kitchen table in Los Angeles, California, and wrote three words at the top of a yellow pad: 'My Life List'."

"On his Life List, John Goddard, an adventurer and explorer, wrote down 127 goals. John is now nearly 75 years old and he has achieved 108 of those goals. Let's look at the type of things that John wrote down."

Fourth Ward Elementary school's local heroes who, like John Goddard, started out with dreams that started them on their journey to their successes.

Procedure:

1) Review the Life List of a Fifteen-year-old.

2) Ask questions about things on the list that are age-appropriate for your students.

Example:

"Can anyone tell me where the Congo River is?"

"Can anyone tell me where Niagara Falls is?"

3) Ask the class to take the list and circle the things that they also would like to do. Tell them to simply skip over the things that they don't understand.

4) Refer to some of the locations in your Geography class. Encourage students to look up the places John wanted to go.

5) Give the students copies of the blank Life List.

   Note: For some early grades, you may have students do illustrations or create a book representing their Life Lists.

6) Have the students write down as many things as they can think of representing things that they would like to do, places they would like to visit, etc. Encourage each student to note at least one thing under each heading.

7) Discuss and display their lists.

Additional Activity

Materials:

Magazines, newspapers, travel brochures, and coloring books.

Procedure:

1) Take the Life Lists and using 8 1/2 by 11 sheets of construction paper create a book of pictures depicting the dreams represented on the lists. Pictures can be illustrated by students or cut out of the newspapers and magazines that you provide.

2) Keep the books in the classroom and add to them throughout the school year.

"Well class, we have identified many of our dreams in life. Now, we simply need to learn as much as we can about how to make these dreams come true."

My Life List

Things that I would like to be able to do:

For example: read, write my name, count money, etc.

Places where I would like to go:

For example: Disneyland, Kenya, France, England

Things that I would like to learn or study:

For example: how to publish a book, how to cook

Things that I would like to accomplish:

For example: Ride an elephant, fly an airplane

Places where I would like to live:

For example: in other states, in other countries

The type of family that I would like to have:

For example: a husband or wife and how many children

Hobbies that I would like to have:

For example: collecting baseball cards, fishing, golf

Changes that I would like to make in the world:

For example: end hunger, protect the whales

People whom I would like to help:

For example: the elderly, the homeless, those who can't read

How I would like people to remember me:

For example: kind, responsible, honest, smart

Life List of a Fifteen-year-old

Explore:
- *1. Nile River
- *2. Amazon River
- *3. Congo River
- *4. Colorado River
- 5. Yangtze River, China
- 6. Niger River
- 7. Orinoco River, Venezuela
- *8. Rio Coco, Nicaragua

Study Cultures In:
- *9. The Congo
- *10. New Guinea
- *11. Brazil
- *12. Borneo
- *13. The Sudan (John was nearly buried alive in a sandstorm.)
- *14. Australia
- *15. Kenya
- *16. The Philippines
- *17. Tanganyika (now Tanzania)
- *18. Ethiopia
- *19. Nigeria
- *20. Alaska

Climb:
- 21. Mount Everest
- 22. Mount Aconcagua, Argentina
- 23. Mount McKinley
- *24. Mount Huascaran, Peru
- *25. Mount Kilimanjaro
- *26. Mount Ararat, Turkey
- *27. Mount Kenya
- 28. Mount Cook, New Zealand
- *29. Mount Popocatepetl, Mexico
- *30. The Matterhorn

---

* Indicates items that have been completed or achieved.

Life List of a Fifteen-year-old (continued)

Climb:

31. Mount Rainier
*32. Mount Fuji
*33. Mount Vesuvius
*34. Mount Bromo, Java
*35. Grand Tetons
*36. Mount Baldy, California

Do:

*37. Carry out careers in medicine and exploration (Studied pre-med and treats illnesses among primitive tribes)
38. Visit every country in the world (30 to go)
*39. Study Navaho and Hopi Indians
*40. Learn to fly a plane
*41. Ride horse in Rose Parade

Photograph:

*42. Iguacu Falls, Brazil
*43. Victoria Falls, Rhodesia (Chased by a warthog in the process)
*44. Sutherland Falls, New Zealand
*45. Yosemite Falls
*46. Niagara Falls
*47. Retrace travels of Marco Polo and Alexander the Great

Explore Underwater:

*48. Coral reefs of Florida
*49. Great Barrier Reef, Australia (Photographed a 300-pound clam)
*50. Red Sea
*51. Fiji Islands
*52. The Bahamas
*53. Explore Okefenokee Swamp and the Everglades

Visit:

54. North and South Poles
*55. Great Wall of China
*56. Panama and Suez Canals

---

* Indicates items that have been completed or achieved.

Life List of a Fifteen-year-old (continued)

Visit (continued):

*57. Easter Island
*58. The Galapagos Islands
*59. Vatican City (Saw the pope)
*60. The Taj Mahal
*61. The Eiffel Tower
*62. The Blue Grotto
*63. The Tower of London
*64. The Leaning Tower of Pisa
*65. The Sacred Well of Chicken-Itza, Mexico
*66. Climb Ayers Rock in Australia
67. Follow River Jordan from Sea of Galilee to Dead Sea
*68. Lake Victoria
*69. Lake Superior
*70. Lake Tanganyika
*71. Lake Titicaca, South America

Accomplish:

*72. Lake Nicaragua
*73. Become an Eagle Scout
*74. Dive in a submarine
*75. Land on and take off from an aircraft carrier
*76. Fly in a blimp, hot air balloon and glider
*77. Ride an elephant, camel, ostrich and bronco
*78. Skin dive to 40 feet and hold breath two and a half minutes underwater
*79. Catch a ten-pound lobster and a ten-inch abalone
*80. Play flute and violin
*81. Type 50 words a minute
*82. Take a parachute jump
*83. Learn water and snow skiing
*84. Go on a church mission
*85. Follow the John Muir Trail
*86. Study native medicines and bring back useful ones

---

* Indicates items that have been completed or achieved.

Life List of a Fifteen-year-old (continued)

Accomplish (continued):

*87. Bag camera trophies of elephant, lion, rhino, cheetah, cape buffalo and whale
*88. Learn to fence
*89. Learn jujitsu
*90. Teach a college course
*91. Watch a cremation ceremony in Bali
*92. Explore depths of the sea
93. Appear in a Tarzan movie (He now considers this an irrelevant boyhood dream)
94. Own a horse, chimpanzee, cheetah, ocelot and coyote (Yet to own a chimp or cheetah)
95. Become a ham radio operator
*96. Build own telescope
*97. Write a book (On Nile trip)
*98. Publish an article in National Geographic Magazine
*99. High jump five feet
*100. Broad jump 15 feet
*101. Run a mile in five minutes
*102. Weigh 175 pounds stripped (still does)
*103. Perform 200 sit-ups and 20 pull-ups
*104. Learn French, Spanish and Arabic
105. Study dragon lizards on Komodo Island (Boat broke down within 20 miles of island)
*106. Visit birthplace of Grandfather Sorenson in Denmark
*107. Visit birthplace of Grandfather Goddard in England
*108. Ship aboard a freighter as a seaman
109. Read the entire Encyclopedia Britannica (Has read extensive parts in each volume)
*110. Read the Bible from cover to cover
*111. Read the works of Shakespeare, Plato, Aristotle, Dickens, Thoreau, Poe, Rousseau, Bacon, Hemingway, Twain, Burroughs, Conrad, Talmage, Tolstoi, Longfellow, Keats, Whittier and Emerson (Not every work of each)

---

* Indicates items that have been completed or achieved.

Life List of a Fifteen-year-old (continued)

Accomplish (continued):

*112. Become familiar with the compositions of Bach, Beethoven, Debussy, Ibert, Mendelssohn, Lalo, Rimski-Korsakov, Respighi, Liszt, Rachmaninoff, Stravinsky, Toch, Tschaikovsky, Verdi

*113. Become proficient in the use of a plane, motorcycle, tractor, surf board, rifle, pistol, canoe, microscope, football, basketball, bow and arrow, lariat and boomerang

*114. Compose music

*115. Play Clair de Lune on the piano

*116. Watch fire-walking ceremony (In Bali and Surinam)

*117. Milk a poisonous snake (Bitten by a diamond back during a photo session)

*118. Light a match with a 22 rifle

*119. Visit a movie studio

*120. Climb Cheops' pyramid

*121. Become a member of the Explorers' Club and the Adventurers' Club

*122. Learn to play polo

*123. Travel through the Grand Canyon on foot and by boat

*124. Circumnavigate the globe (four times)

125. Visit the moon ("Someday if God wills")

*126. Marry and have children (Has five children)

127. Live to see the 21st Century (He will be 75)

— Taken from *Chicken Soup for the Soul*

----

* Indicates items that have been completed or achieved.

Activity 35

Things We Dream of Doing

Objectives

- To provide a visual reference of your students' Life Lists.

- To provide an activity for the entire school staff.

- To provide a visual reference of students and staff for achieving goals throughout the school year.

Materials

- Construction paper.
- Scissors.

Procedure:

1) Create a bulletin board called "Things We Dream of Doing" for your students in your classroom and one for the staff elsewhere in the school, perhaps in the main corridor.

2) Get a camera and take a picture of each student in your classroom.

3) Have a student of group of students take pictures of everyone on the school staff. Have them give a copy of the the lists from the previous Activity to complete.

4) Gather all of the student lists together with their pictures and post on your "Things We Dream of Doing" bulletin board.

5) Instruct your students to place a check mark next to any item that they achieve during this school year.

6) Gather all of the lists from the school staff and attach each list along with their picture to a sheet of construction paper.

7) Post the sheets to the Things We Dream of Doing bulletin board for staff.

8) Instruct the staff to place a check mark next to each item on their lists, that they have already achieved or that they achieve during the school year.

Students at Welborn Elementary School have Big Plans for their future!

Teachers have dreams too!

A Dream Cluster celebrates both dreams and diversity.

Wynn/Blassie • © 1995 Rising Sun Publishing • (800) 524-2813
Building Dreams: Elementary School Edition Teacher's Guide

Activity 36

When I Graduate From Elementary School

Objectives

- To help students focus on the types of things they would like to do after they acquire their education.
- To help students internalize the relevance of education in achieving their dreams and aspirations.

Materials

- Construction paper.
- Scissors.
- Camera.

A special thank you to Maria Ybarra, a fifth grade teacher at Beaverbrook Elementary school in Griffin, Georgia, for sharing this activity.

"Class, I would like for you to think about what you're going to do when you graduate from elementary school. I would imagine that all of you will be going to middle school, to high school, maybe to undergraduate school, perhaps on to medical school, law school, or graduate school. Some of you may intend to go on to get a Ph.D. We're going to write different papers regarding the different types of things we would like to do after we graduate. First, we will write about the other schools and types of education we would like to continue in. Later, we will write about places to go, things to see, and so on."

Procedure:

1) Take pictures of your students dressed in caps and gowns.

2) Post the pictures onto a bulletin board (e.g., "When I Graduate. . .").

3) Place captions beneath each photo (e.g., Dr. Jones, I plan to travel around the world, etc.).

4) Have your students write a paper about the schools they plan to attend after graduating from elementary school.

5) Post the papers onto the bulletin board.

6) Continue the activity with papers about where they would like to go, what type of careers they would like, where they would like to live, etc.

7) Gather the papers together to create a "When I Graduate" book.

Force of habit rules the hallways and classrooms. Neither brain science nor education research has been able to free the majority of America's schools from their 19th-century roots. If more administrators were tuned into brain research, scientists argue, not only would schedules change, but subjects such as foreign language and geometry would be offered to much younger children. Music and gym would be daily requirements. Lectures, work sheets and rote memorization would be replaced by hands-on materials, drama and project work.

— Lynnell Hancock, *Why Do Schools Flunk Biology?*

Activity 37

Character Values

Objectives

- To help students develop important life skills.
- To help students internalize character values and behaviors consistent with achieving their dreams and aspirations.
- To help students make positive choices when confronted with personal conflicts and negative peer pressures.

Materials

- Construction paper.
- Scissors.

A special thank you to Linda McKay for sharing her thoughts on character education. Linda is the coordinator of the Personal Responsibility Education Process in St. Louis, Missouri, through the Network of Cooperating Schools.

There are fifteen character values that we discuss in our classroom throughout the school year. We talk about them every day. The students are continually being encouraged to think about, internalize, act out, and recognize the traits in others. We discuss the character values regularly and apply them to situations that occur in the classroom.

One day I saw a student who found some money and gave it to me. I shared the experience with the class and I asked, "What character value was just demonstrated?" The students made several insightful comments about personal responsibility, integrity, and trustworthiness. They knew the values.

When such traits as respect, responsibility, honesty, cooperation, caring, etc., are experienced, they not only form positive memory tapes, but they fuel the decisions and actions of a lifetime and create the foundation for the memory tapes of the next generation. When you come into our room my students can tell you what integrity means, what the fifteen values are and why they are important to the society.

Students are caring and eager to cooperate. When someone is struggling, everyone wants to help that student. We are a caring Dream Classroom and we want to assist anyone who needs help. Students care more about each other.

When reading stories, what character values did the main character have? What character values could the main character have had that would have changed the story?

Eighteen years ago, if you walked into *my* classroom, you could have heard a pin drop. Everybody had to sit in their seats, they had to face the front, and work only on their own papers. But not today. There's a lot of learning going on. Cooperation, working with someone in their groups by asking how to use a thesaurus, or dictionary, or help with a math problem, how to pronounce a word, etc., creates a partnership. This is what you witness in *our* classroom.

At the start of school, I proudly display the fifteen character values in the room. I refer to them on a daily basis and, of course, it is very important to explain these to the parents at Open House. If a child has a problem, we discuss as a group the character value that he/she was having difficulty with and what we can do to prepare him/her to become successful.

Procedure:

1) Post each of the character values around the room.

2) Discuss one value at the beginning of the school day.

Example:

"Class today's character value is 'integrity.' Who would like to tell me what integrity means?"

"Who would like to give us an example of when integrity is being displayed?"

"See if you can compliment someone on how they display integrity today."

3) Write the character value on the board.

4) "Class, think of one way in which you can display this character value in pursuing your dreams."

5) "Think of one story that you've read recently where one of the characters either displayed integrity or lacked integrity."

6) "Write down on a sheet of paper how the character displayed integrity or lacked integrity."

The *Child Development Project* of Oakland, California, defines a family environment for our children as:

. . .a community where care and trust are emphasized above restrictions and threats, where unity and pride (of accomplishment and in purpose) replace winning and losing, and where each person is asked, helped, and inspired to live up to such ideals and values as kindness, fairness, and responsibility. [Such] a classroom community seeks to meet each student's need to feel competent, connected to others, and autonomous.

. . .Students are not only exposed to basic human values, they also have many opportunities to think about, discuss, and act on those values, while gaining experiences that promote empathy and understanding of others.

Activity 38

Let Me Tell You All About Me

Objectives

- To guide students through a number of activities in which they write, speak, and share information about themselves.

- To help students discover their dreams and aspirations.

- To help students increase their language and writing skills as they share their stories, dreams, and aspirations with others.

Materials

- Internet access or postage and envelopes.

The process of discovering dreams and aspirations occurs in many activities during a person's time in school. However, we often miss the crystallizing or "Aha" experience, the moment that a person really learns and often decides to pursue extended study, or the experience that inspires a person to pursue a career or area of interest.

Thomas Armstrong, in <u>Awakening Your Child's Natural Genius</u>, notes:

> For violin great Yehudi Menuhin, the crystallizing experience came when his parents took him to see the San Francisco Symphony Orchestra as a three-year-old. This experience so enthralled him that he asked to be given a violin as well as lessons with the orchestra's principal violinist. His parents provided both. In Albert Einstein's case, the turning point was when his father presented him with a simple scientific instrument that evoked his curiosity. "A wonder of such nature I experienced as a child of 4 or 5 when my father showed me a compass," recalled Einstein. "That this needle behaved in such a determined way did not at all fit into the nature of events. . . I can still remember—or at least believe I can remember—that this experience made a deep and lasting impression upon me."

In each instance, family members provided simple resources, seemingly innocent in themselves, that had a powerful emotional impact upon these creative individuals, pulling them along a path of development that ultimately led to their major life accomplishments.

Thomas Armstrong, in <u>In Their Own Way</u> cites:

> By the age of twelve, Chris was managing two profitable businesses at home and had a one-man art show at his elementary school. At five, Justin was giving talks on the solar system, creating elaborate Lego structures, and writing and illustrating his own original stories. Marc was an eleven-year-old Dungeons and Dragons expert, widely read on the subject. He also created animated movies. All three of these boys were labeled learning disabled by their school districts and forced to attend special remedial classes at their respective schools.

Keep note paper at your desk. Look for the "Aha" experiences. Communicate your observations to parents. Help them to help their child discover his/her dreams and aspirations.

> When a baby comes into the world her brain is a jumble of neurons, all waiting to be woven into the intricate tapestry of the mind. Trillions upon trillions of neurons are more like the Pentium chips in a computer before the factory preloads the software. They are pure and of almost infinite potential. It is the experiences of childhood, determining which neurons are used, that wire the circuits of the brain. . . which experiences a child has—determines whether the child grows up to be intelligent or dull, fearful or self-assured, articulate or tongue-tied. Early experiences are so powerful, says pediatric neuro-biologist Harry Chugani of Wayne State University, that "they can completely change the way a person turns out."
>
> — Sharon Begley, *Your Child's Brain*

"Class, we are going to work on some writing activities that we will eventually share with others either via the Internet or by actually mailing our letters, stories, and other writing activities to other students in different parts of the country and even the world."

"What do you think are some of the first questions other children would want to ask you?"

"Well, they would want to know your name, how old you are, where you live and where you go to school. They might like to know something about your family and what types of things you like to do."

Procedure:

1) Identify a school in your area or contact our offices to connect with a school in another part of the country (800) 524-2813. Once you are connected with a similar grade-level teacher have the teacher engage his/her students in the same activity and announce to the students that they will be sharing letters either by mail or via Internet.

2) Have your students write a paper answering the following questions:

   A. My name is. . .

   B. I am _____ years old.

   C. I am in the _____ grade and I attend _____.

   D. I have _____ brothers and _____ sisters.

   E. Their names are _____ and they are _____ years old.

   F. Some of the things that I like to do are _____.

   G. Some of the things that I like about my school are _____.

   H. Some of the things that I would like to do in the future are _____.

3) Have each student read his/her letter to the class.

4) Send letters and express to the teacher on the receiving end to try to match students by similar areas of interest.

5) Students' responses from the other school should follow the same format.

   Note: This activity can also be performed with foreign language students.

Activity 39

MY DREAM

Objectives

- To help students process the information that they have been discussing relating to their dreams.

- To enhance language skills.

Materials

- MY DREAM sheets.
- Construction paper.

"Class, we're going to do an activity entitled 'MY DREAM.' We're going to take each letter in the words MY DREAM and write each letter on a line and use the letter to begin a sentence that describes our dream, something about our dream, something that we will have to do to achieve our dream or something that describes the character of someone who achieves his/her dream."

"After we complete our dream papers, we are going to write a letter to our parents explaining our dream paper and why we have that type of dream."

Procedure:

1) Have students write MY DREAM on a sheet of notebook paper, writing one letter on each line (or use the MY DREAM sheet on the following page).

2) Have students write a sentence using the first letter on each line.

Example:

My dream is to become a writer.
Your dreams can only be achieved through hard work.

Determination is important to achieving your dreams.
Respect others so that they can have dreams too.
Education teaches you how to achieve your dreams.
Always giving your best prepares you to achieve your dreams.
Many people have dreams, but many people quit before they achieve their dreams.

3) Have students paste their papers onto sheets of construction paper. Cut and color the construction paper into rainbows, clouds, stars, or other creative images.

4) Have students write a letter about their dream paper to their parents describing their dream and why they have this particular dream.

Student: _____ Date: _____

M _____

_____

Y _____

_____

D _____

_____

R _____

_____

E _____

_____

A _____

_____

M _____

_____

Activity 40

Let Me Tell You About My Dreams

Objectives

- To guide students through a number of activities in which they write, speak, and share information about things that they dream of doing.

- To help students increase their language and writing skills as they share their dreams, and aspirations with others.

Materials

- Internet access or postage and envelopes.

This activity helps students to further explore the types of things they like to do. These may not be considered dreams and aspirations. Simply enjoyable things, i.e., hobbies, special interests, etc.

"Class, we are going to spend some time focusing on some of the things that we really like to do. It may be collecting baseball cards, going to museums, drawing, playing sports, writing poetry, pretending to be a teacher or parent, or experimenting with cooking exotic foods. Whatever it is, this is something that *you* like to do. It doesn't matter if anyone else wants to do it. These are the special things that you like to do."

Students weave a quilt of dreams.

Procedure:

1) Have your students write a paper, a poem, or a story answering the following questions:

   A. My name is _____. This is my dream paper.

   B. What are some of the things that you dream of doing?

   C. What would be your dream job, why?

   D. What would your dream house look like, why?

   E. What would be some of the dream things that you would own like cars, boats, airplanes, clothes, jewelry, etc.?

   F. What would your dream world be like?

   For example:

   How would people treat each other?

   What would the world's environment be like?

   What languages would they speak?

   What would be the state of war, poverty, and crime?

   G. What would your dream family be like?

   H. What type of schools would your children go to?

   I. What type of things would you do with your dream family?

   J. What type of hobbies would you have?

   K. What type of friends would you have?

2) What are some of the dream places that you would like to go?

   For example:

   Would you like to go to a foreign country?

   Would you like to visit the President in the White House?

   Would you like to go to an expensive restaurant?

   Would you like to see how a great chef prepares a meal?

   Would you like to visit a particular college or university?

   Would you like to go to sporting events like the Super Bowl or the NBA Basketball championship game, or the Wimbledon Tennis Finals, or the Olympics?

3) Have each student read his/her letter to the class.

4) Have your students share these letters with their pen pals.

Activity 41

How to Make My Dreams Come True

Objectives

- To guide students through a number of research activities in which they research their dreams and aspirations.

- To help students increase higher-order thinking and language skills as they share their research activities.

- To help students gain an understanding of the practical planning process of identifying a dream and identifying the steps necessary to achieve the dream.

Materials

- Internet access or postage and envelopes.

"Class, now that we have focused on the types of things that we like to do, we are going to identify the types of things we will have to do to achieve our dreams and aspirations. This is the difference between wishing or daydreaming and really believing that our dreams and aspirations can become a reality."

"For example, if someone wanted a dream house, what would be the steps necessary to making that dream house a reality?"

"Identify what the house would look like, draw up plans, identify the types of materials, how much it will cost, who will actually build it, where to get the money to pay for construction (i.e., Will we have all of the money or will we have to apply for a mortgage loan), what color the house will be, what type of furnishings will be put into the house, where will the house be located, etc."

"Class, this is called brainstorming. We identify something that we want to do. We identified the steps that are necessary to achieve it. We then engage in a discussion with other people in which we identify some additional steps that we may need to take to achieve this dream."

"Let's take a moment and think about some of the other ways we could gather information about how to turn our dreams into reality in addition to brainstorming?"

We Learn by Doing

Not many years ago I began to play the cello. Most people would say that what I am doing is "learning to play" the cello. But these words carry into our minds the strange idea that there exists two very different processes: (1) learning to play the cello; and (2) playing the cello. They imply that I will do the first until I have completed it, at which point I will stop the first process and begin the second. In short, I will go on "learning to play" until I have "learned to play" and then I will begin to play. Of course, this is nonsense. There are not two processes, but one. We learn to do something by doing it. There is no other way.

— John Holt, *How Children Fail*

Procedure:

1) Have each student select from their Dreams List [or Life Lists] a dream in each of the following categories:

   A. A place where they would like to go.

   B. A food that they've never tasted that they would like to taste.

   C. A change that they would like to see in their school.

2) Have each student take sheets of paper and list all of the things that they think they'll have to do to make that dream a reality.

3) Have one student share one of his/her dreams with the class.

4) Ask the class to think about the things that would be necessary to achieve this dream.

5) Have the student share the things they thought of.

6) Have a discussion with the class about the additional things they thought of that the student may have missed.

7) Have the student add to his/her list.

8) Repeat the exercise with each student in the classroom.

9) Hold a discussion about the other sources of information available to your students to facilitate identifying the steps necessary to achieve their dreams.

For example:

- Libraries
- Mentors
- U.S. Government Information Offices
- School Alumni
- Trade periodicals, books, magazines

10) Instruct your students to take their dream papers and list all of the things that they will need to do to make each dream a reality.

11) Post the student dreams on a bulletin board under their respective categories.

12) Gather papers together based upon like interests, e.g., all students who want to taste French food, Mexican food, etc. All of the students who want to travel to European countries, African countries, or other cities within the United States, etc.

13) Take some of the papers and engage in a classroom discussion about how students can turn their dreams into goals. Break down how to identify the steps necessary to achieve their goals.

Example:

"Class, let's identify the steps necessary to achieve our goal of traveling to France. For example, we need a passport, we need to identify our method of travel (e.g., plane, cruise ship, freighter, etc.), how much each fare will cost, what the weather is like during the time that we wish to travel, French currency, exchange rate, the U.S. Embassy location, etc."

14) Put these papers on the bulletin board together with the steps identified to achieve the goal and allow students to work independently on the research activities needed to achieve the respective steps. Take some of the goals and allow students to select the steps that they will work on.

Example:

"Who is willing to research what it takes to get a passport? Who is willing to get travel brochures to France? Who is willing to research how much it will cost to fly, to take a cruise, to take a freighter, etc?"

15) As information is gathered, place a note together with the student's name onto the bulletin board until all of the steps have been researched.

The successful student is one who learns how to use research materials, libraries, note cards, and computer files, as well as knowledgeable parents, teachers, older students, and classmates, in order to master those tasks of schools that are not transparently clear. In a terminology that has recently become fashionable, intelligence is "distributed" in the environment as well as in the head, and the "intelligent student" makes use of the intelligence distributed throughout his environment.

In his commentary on conventional schools Dr. Gardner comments:

. . . in those instances where the schooling is uninspired, where the masters are such in name only, or where the graduates go on to pursue vocations unrelated to the curriculum of the school, one may question whether the knowledge and skills attained will prove of value to the students or to the society that has entrusted them to the institution called school.

— Howard Gardner, *The Unschooled Mind: How Children Think & How Schools Should Teach*

Activity 42

Things I Want To Learn

Objectives

- To listen to the unique and changing areas of interest of your students.

- To provide a visual reference of student interests.

- To raise comprehension and higher-order thinking as students gather and share information beyond the scope of the curriculum.

- To provide students with an opportunity to engage in expanded reading, writing, and research activities.

Materials

- Bulletin board.

"Class, in addition to the things that we are required to learn by the school district, there may be other things that we want to learn about. For example, some of you may be interested in writing and publishing a book. We would need to do some additional things to help you learn how to publish a book. Some of you may be interested in attending Space Camp. We would have to write letters and gather information regarding how much it would cost to attend and what dates Space Camp will be offered."

"We are going to create a special bulletin board where you can post the additional things that you would like to learn. We, as a class, will put our minds together to discover how we can learn about these things together."

A bulletin board invite students to dream and learn.

Procedure:

1) Create a special bulletin board where you can post student ideas about "The Things That I Would Like To Learn."

2) Have students post their ideas and areas of interest on the board throughout the school year. They may include places that they want to go, guest speakers that they want to hear, etc.

3) Provide an area of the board or a folder for students to place articles, brochures, or other types of information regarding the areas of interest.

4) Conduct an activity that introduces students to research steps, such as:

"Amie wants to become a pediatrician. What are some of the sources of information for Amie?"

    A. Amie's research should include:
- Medical Schools
- Grants/Scholarships
- Professional Medical Associations
- Medical Conferences
- Student or Junior Medical Organizations
- Medical publications
- Local Hospitals
- Local Mentoring Organizations
- Medical-related articles published in local newspapers
- High Schools with Medical Dream Teams or clubs

    B. Amie could write papers on:
- Pediatric Care
- Why I want to become a Doctor
- How I can benefit my community by becoming a Doctor
- The outlook for Doctors in the year 2020
- Private practice versus HMO's

    C. Amie could interview doctors and write letters to local pediatricians in search of mentorship.

5) All of the information gathered is to be posted to the "What I Would Like To Learn" bulletin board.

6) Gather the information for each area of interests into a folder or binder to become a reference source.

7) On each binder, paper, article, or information source give individual students credit for having contributed the information into the class reference book.

Example:

The following article on Pediatric Medicine was contributed by Brittany Pyles on May 1, 1995.

The following brochures on Franchise opportunities were gathered and submitted by Matt Polynce on February 10, 1995.

8) Have students create a biographical page for each reference source that they contribute from.

9) Have students organize their classroom research and reference library so that they can share their information with other classes and visitors.

Activity 43

My Dream Collage

Objectives

- To help students process what they've learned about their dreams.
- To provide students with a convenient place to store their dream papers, research information, and activities.

Materials

- Poster board.
- Construction paper.
- Newspapers/magazines.
- Personal photos.
- Travel brochures.
- Glue.
- Glitter.
- Markers.

"Class, today we're going to create a collage of our dreams. On your collage, you may want to place pictures of what your dream house, car, bedroom, and so forth, will look like. You may want to cut out or write dream-building and eagle words, and character values that could be used to describe the type of person that you will become as you achieve your dreams. You may want to place pictures or words describing the types of things that you like to do or the things that you will have to do to achieve your dreams; for example, graduating from college, investing in stocks and bonds, traveling, learning foreign languages, running for political office and so forth."

"You may want to draw pictures of people holding hands if you dream of a caring and safe world. Our completed collages will be displayed throughout the school."

Procedure:

1) Have students cut out photos, words, phrases, articles, etc., related to achieving their dreams.

   These can include such things that have already been taught such as:

   - Character Values

   - Eagle Words and phrases

   - Personal photos

   - Dream houses, bedrooms, kitchens, etc.

   - Places that they would like to visit

   - Hobbies that they would like to pursue

2) Have students paste their words, photos, etc., to their poster boards. Encourage students to use their creativity in writing, gluing, using glitter, etc., to decorate their collages.

Activity 44

Mid-Year Student Assessment

Objectives

- To assess student attitudes regarding school.
- To assess the extent to which students have focused on their dreams and aspirations.

Materials

- Student Assessment forms.

"To help me prepare you to become successful I need you to think about what you've learned so far this school year about things related to your dreams and aspirations."

"This is not a test. There are no right or wrong answers. I just want you to honestly answer the questions as best you can."

"If I am a successful teacher, then all of you will have dreams and aspirations by the end of the school year and I will have taught you many things that will help you to achieve your dreams and aspirations."

Procedure:

1) Distribute the survey sheets and discuss the questions with your students. In the early grades, a classroom discussion may replace the individual surveys.

2) Have students complete the survey sheets.

3) Have a classroom activity where students help you tally the responses to the survey.

For example:

Divide the students into groups and distribute several completed survey forms to each group. Have each group log the responses to several questions.

"Group one, tally the answers to questions 1, 2, and 3. Group two, tally the answers to questions 4, 5, and 6, etc."

4) From the lists of responses discuss some of the responses each day. Discuss the steps the class might take to help satisfy some of the needs and to overcome some of the obstacles confronting students. By this time, all of the dreams and aspirations of your students should have been discussed, illustrated, or written about in one or more of the activities. However, if some of the responses indicated new dreams, make sure that these are posted somewhere in the classroom.

Student Survey

Instructions: Take a moment to think about how you feel about school.

1. List two of your dreams and aspirations.

_____
_____
_____

2. List three things that you have learned in school this year that are related to your dreams and aspirations.

_____
_____
_____

3. List three classes or activities in this school that are helping you toward achieving your dreams and aspirations.

_____
_____
_____

4. What was the *best* activity or project that you were involved in this year?

_____
_____

Building Dreams: Elementary School Edition © 1995 RISING SUN PUBLISHING (800) 524-2813

Student Survey (continued)

Instructions: Take a moment to think about how you would like for school to help you achieve your goals in life.

5. Are there things in this classroom that interfere with or hinder you from achieving your dreams and aspirations?

_____
_____
_____
_____

6. List three things that your parents, teachers, and/or other students do to help you feel good about yourself.

_____
_____
_____
_____

7. Describe three ways that your parents, teachers, or other students are supportive of your dreams and aspirations.

_____
_____
_____
_____

Building Dreams: Elementary School Edition © 1995 RISING SUN PUBLISHING (800) 524-2813

Student Survey (continued)

Instructions: Take a moment to think about how you would like for school to help you achieve your goals in life.

8. Describe the types of things that your parents, teachers and/or other students do that hurt your feelings or cause you to feel badly about yourself.

_____
_____
_____
_____
_____

9. Describe the types of things that your parents, teachers, or other students do that interfere with or hinder you from achieving your dreams and aspirations.

_____
_____
_____
_____
_____
_____
_____

Building Dreams: Elementary School Edition © 1995 RISING SUN PUBLISHING (800) 524-2813

Student Survey (continued)

Instructions: Take a moment to think about how you would like for school to help you achieve your goals in life.

10. What is your favorite part of the school day? Why?

___

11. What is your favorite class? Why?

___

12. Describe any special clubs or activities that you are involved in that are helping you to pursue your dreams.

___

Building Dreams: Elementary School Edition © 1995 RISING SUN PUBLISHING (800) 524-2813

Teacher Survey

1. Based on the dreams and aspirations of our students, what additional areas of knowledge do our students need to acquire?

_____
_____
_____
_____
_____
_____
_____

2. What types of people, training, programs, materials, or technology do we need to help our students acquire these areas of knowledge?

_____
_____
_____
_____
_____
_____
_____
_____

Teacher Survey (continued)

3. In what ways can we present, teach, provide exposure to and experience with these areas of knowledge so that all of our students have the best opportunity to achieve their dreams?

_____

_____

_____

_____

_____

4. What additional resources do we need in our school/community to help our students acquire the knowledge and experiences that they need?

_____

_____

_____

_____

_____

_____

_____

_____

I Am A Teacher

I am a Teacher.

I was born the first moment that a question leaped from the mouth of a child.

I have been many people in many places.

I am Socrates exciting the youth of Athens to discover new ideas through the use of questions.

I am Anne Sullivan tapping out the secrets of the universe into the outstretched hand of Helen Keller.

I am Aesop and Hans Christian Andersen revealing truth through countless stories.

I am Marva Collins fighting for every child's right to an education.

I am Mary McCleod Bethune building a great college for my people, using orange crates for desks.

And I am Bel Kaufman struggling to go Up The Down Staircase.

The names of those who have practiced my profession ring like a hall of fame for humanity. . . Booker T. Washington, Buddha, Confucius, Ralph Waldo Emerson, Leo Buscaglia, Moses and Jesus. . .

— John W. Schlatter, *Chicken Soup for the Soul*

Activity 45

Apprenticeships/Mentors

Objectives

- To teach students how to identify people or organizations that can help them achieve their dreams and aspirations.
- To enhance language and writing skills.
- To enhance research and personal presentations skills.

Materials

- Copies of student activity sheets.
- Envelopes.
- Stamps.

"To help prepare ourselves to become successful we need to identify people, businesses, organizations, schools, and programs where we can learn more about how to achieve our dreams and gain experience doing the things that we like to do."

"For example, students who have dreams and aspirations related to art might identify professional artists who could teach them more about art, design, layout, paste-up, and the art industry. They might identify schools that specialize in art. They might identify after-school programs that teach art. They might identify architectural, drafting, or drawing programs. They might identify computer programs that teach art. They might identify video tapes that teach art. They might also identify an art teacher who is willing to tutor them or work with them outside of regular classroom time."

Procedure:

1) Have your students take the form in this section to the library to research each question. Instruct them to use additional paper if necessary.

 "Class, we are going to identify one dream that we would like to achieve and write it at the top of the sheet of paper that I am distributing. Then, we are going to the library to research each question. Be sure to note the telephone numbers and addresses of all of the people, businesses, programs, schools, and so forth that we can identify that can help us learn more about our dreams."

2) Organize students into groups with similar dreams and conduct a classroom activity where students in each group address envelopes to the people, businesses, organizations, programs, etc., that they have researched. Only one letter should be sent to a person or organization.

3) Create a master letter for each category of dreams, e.g., medicine, law, art, education, entrepreneurship, etc.

4) Make as many copies as you need so that you can enclose one in each envelope and mail to the people and organizations that your students have identified.

5) Create a folder with copies of your letters and a folder for responses received.

When I was young and free and my imagination had no limits, I dreamed of changing the world. As I grew older and wiser, I discovered the world would not change, so I shortened my sights somewhat and decided to change only my country.

But it, too, seemed immovable.

As I grew into my twilight years, in one last desperate attempt, I settled for changing only my family, those closest to me, but alas, they would have none of it.

And now as I lie on my deathbed, I suddenly realize:

If I had only changed myself first,

then by example I would have changed my family.

From their inspiration and encouragement, I would then have been able to better my country and, who knows, I may have even changed the world.

– Anonymous

Student: _____

Write down one of the dreams and aspirations that you would like to learn more about:
_____
_____

List the names and addresses of all of the people who could give you more information about this dream:
_____
_____
_____
_____
_____

List all of the special programs or activities that could teach you more about this dream:
_____
_____
_____
_____
_____
_____

Building Dreams: Elementary School Edition © 1995 RISING SUN PUBLISHING (800) 524-2813

Student: _____

List all of the books, magazines, and videotapes that could teach you more about this dream:

_____
_____
_____
_____
_____

List all of the businesses, organizations, or schools that could teach you more about this dream:

_____
_____
_____
_____
_____
_____
_____

Building Dreams: Elementary School Edition © 1995 RISING SUN PUBLISHING (800) 524-2813

Student: _____

List all of the resources on the Internet and World-Wide Web that could teach you more about this dream:

_____
_____
_____
_____
_____
_____
_____

List all of the resources within your school or school district that could teach you more about this dream:

_____
_____
_____
_____
_____
_____
_____

Building Dreams: Elementary School Edition © 1995 RISING SUN PUBLISHING (800) 524-2813

Sample Letter

Dear _____,

Several of our students have indicated a desire to:

_____

In our classroom we believe in helping each other to discover, define, develop, and pursue our dreams and aspirations. We are contacting individuals, schools, businesses, and organizations whom we believe can guide us toward realizing our dreams and aspirations. If you, or someone you know, could offer us advice, insight, or information that would help us, we would surely appreciate it.

We are especially in need of apprenticeship opportunities. Dr. Howard Gardner of Harvard University in his book, *The Unschooled Mind: How Children Think and How Schools Should Teach*, writes:

Indeed, apprenticeships may well be the means of instruction that builds most effectively on the ways in which most young people learn. Such forms of instruction are heavily punctuated with sensorimotor experiences and with the contextualized use of first-order forms of symbolization, such as natural language and simple drawings and gestures.

We believe that if our students find apprenticeship opportunities or mentors, they will be eager to learn more about the areas in which they have dreams and aspirations. These experiences will not only help them to become better students, but they will gain invaluable insight and experiences that will serve them well for a lifetime.

Thank you kindly for your consideration.

Sincerely,

Activity 46

The Dream Tree

Objectives

- To raise self esteem by visually affirming individual student dreams.

- To provide a visual reference of Dream-Building activities.

- To provide a visual reference for reminding students of behavior consistent with achieving individual dreams and aspirations.

Materials

- Construction paper or sign board.

A special thank you to Wanda Johnson, a sixth grade language arts and social studies teacher at Felton Laboratory School, for sharing this activity.

"Class, we've been discussing your dreams and aspirations. Let's create a Dream Tree for our life's goals, the types of things that we want to become, and the types of things that we must do to prepare ourselves."

After several class sessions of discussing what they wanted to become and the types of things that each of them must do to best prepare themselves the students wrote their names and dreams onto leaves which were displayed all year long in our classroom.

This was a very positive activity. Students often went to the Tree and looked at the leaves. Students from other classes also came in to view the Tree. The Tree served as a visual reminder of what students were to accomplish. Also, when students asked why they had to do certain tasks, I could use the Dream Tree as a reminder of why certain tasks were important and that these tasks were consistent with what they had affirmed that they wanted to achieve.

Dreams lead students to becoming Disciplinary experts

Intuitive learner (sometimes known as the natural, naive, or universal learner), the young child who is superbly equipped to learn language and other symbolic systems.

Traditional student (or scholastic learner), the youngster from age seven to age twenty, roughly, who seeks to master the literacies, concepts, and disciplinary forms of the school.

Disciplinary expert (or skilled person), an individual of any age who has mastered the concepts and skills of a discipline or domain and can apply such knowledge appropriately in new situations. Included in the ranks of the disciplinary experts are those students who are able to use the knowledge of their physics class or their history class to illuminate new phenomena. Their knowledge is not limited to the usual test-and-test setting, and they are eligible to enter the ranks of those who "really" understand.

— Howard Gardner, *The Unschooled Mind How Children Learn and How Schools Should Teach*

Activity 47

Dream Team Board

Objectives

- To examine career aspirations.
- To enhance writing skills.
- To structure cooperative learning groups.

Materials

- Newspapers.
- Magazines.
- Camera.
- Construction paper or sign board.

"To help you to become successful, we want to provide you with a support group to help you build your dream. In your special dream group, you will be involved in activities to help your dream to become a reality."

Group students by areas of interest and then into groups of four.

As we prepare our students to become successful, we can help them to experience success in the steps toward achieving their dreams. What types of things do they want to accomplish? What are some of the places that they want to go? What are some of the things that they want to see, careers that they want to engage in, changes that they want to make in their communities and in the world around them? How can we help them experience success in the small steps taken in working towards their dreams?

Our Dream Team boards can represent many different things for our students:

- Careers
- Changes in the environment
- Changes in local or national politics
- Places to go
- Foods to taste
- Languages to speak
- Special hobbies or interests
- Things like cars, homes, and clothing.

Procedure:

1) Gather students into groups based upon their dream career goals.

2) Provide them with newspapers, magazines, construction paper, etc.

3) "Each group is responsible for cutting out articles, photographs, words, and so forth, relating to your dream careers. Using the construction paper, you may also draw, cut out shapes, or write words that you will use in your dream career."

    "Give me some examples of words a doctor would use? What about an airline pilot?"

4) Have students write a paper titled, "Why I want to be. . . "

5) Post the words, illustrations, articles, and papers outside your classroom.

6) Take a photograph of each student.

7) Create Dream Team Boards or corners around the room that represent the various areas of dreams and aspirations. The easiest boards to create will represent careers, e.g.,:

    - Science and Medicine
    - Professional Sports
    - Teaching/Education
    - Writers/Artists

8) Post the photographs onto the dream boards under their respective areas of interest.

9) As students gather articles, papers, books, etc., related to the various dreams, allow them to post them onto the Dream Team Boards.

Children spend their time, not hunched over worksheets, but actively involved in reading and writing about things that **passionately concern** them. They read *real* books—classic children's literature, adventure stories, poetry, how-to-do-it books, current events—not artificially contrived textbooks that lack controversy, conflict, and character development. Kids learn about language by *using* it every day in meaningful ways rather than by completing disconnected assignments bearing little relationship to real-life activities.

In the kindergarten classrooms at PS 192 in New York City, for example, words are everywhere—on the windows, doors, floors, and chalkboards. Every child has his or her own special collection of favorite words, such as *helicopter* and *television*—words far too difficult to be used in a typical basal reader or phonics program but easily mastered by children when the words arise from their own personal interests and concerns. Kids dictate stories to the teacher and have them bound into little books that they can then read along with trade books in the classroom library.

Providing children with the time and resources to explore reading and writing in meaningful ways appears to pay off in improved achievement levels. By the end of the year at PS 192, all 225 kindergartners could read their own dictated stories as well as simple examples of children's literature. Some were even reading on a second-grade level.

— Thomas Armstrong, *Awakening Your Child's Natural Genius*

Activity 48

Guest Speaker Wall of Fame

Objectives

- To provide a special location for posting information regarding the guest speakers who share with your class throughout the year.

- To provide a place for developing a resource library of information and audio and video tapes of guest speakers and their presentations.

- To share the celebrity status that your class bestows upon those who come to share their dreams and aspirations with visitors to your classroom.

Materials

- Construction paper.
- Scissors.
- Boarder.

Guest speakers can make a powerful impact upon students and can provide an important and informative supplemental instructional activity. They can also provide a rare opportunity for students to meet, greet, and ask questions of someone who may be living their dream. Students are introduced to various areas of interest, individual struggles, how people overcame hardships and challenges, and how expertise and individual skills can be applied.

Our Guest Speaker Wall of fame is designed to formally recognize those who have come to share with our class. Our guest speakers represent the dreams and aspirations of our students and expose them to important character values, responsible choices, and a broad range of special interests and career opportunities.

"Class, this year we are going to have some special guests visit our classroom and share their dreams and aspirations with us. We are going to try to select persons who represent each of our dreams and aspirations to come and speak to our class."

"After each guest speaker visits our school, we are going to write a paper about what they talked about and what we learned. I'm going to post one of your papers following each guest speaker on the Guest Speaker Wall of Fame so that by the end of the year we will have a paper about each of our guest speakers."

"We also have a special place for keeping video and/or audio tapes of each guest speaker so that you can listen to the speaker again, later in the school year."

Procedure:

1) Create a special bulletin board for posting student papers about each of your guest speakers.

2) Create a special corner (or the center) of the bulletin board to recognize the current guest speaker. This is where you will post the speaker's photo, biography, or other pertinent information.

3) Send each of your guest speakers thank you letters from your students.

Sample letter to invite speakers to your classroom

Dear _____,

    We are building dreams in our classroom. Our students will be discussing, exploring, and researching their dreams and aspirations throughout the school year. We are always interested in having people like you share insight, information, experiences, and pitfalls encountered in pursuing their own dreams and aspirations.

    The pursuit of your career may be a dream in itself or it may be a vehicle to pursue other dreams in life such as lifestyle, family, places to go, things to do, addressing important societal issues, etc.

    Our class would really appreciate the opportunity of listening to and asking questions of you.

    If you can visit our classroom as a guest speaker during the school year, please indicate three dates that you will be available to come:

    Date: _____ Circle preferred time: AM or PM

    Date: _____ Circle preferred time: AM or PM

    Date: _____ Circle preferred time: AM or PM

    Attached is a list of the types of questions that our students will be prepared to ask you.

    Sincerely,

Some of the questions that we ask our guest speakers

1) How old were you when you first decided to pursue your dream job?

2) How old were you when you first realized that you had a special talent for doing what you do?

3) What were some of the challenges and obstacles that you had to overcome?

4) Was there any special experience or person who helped you to decide to do what you do?

5) Who were the most influential people in your life who helped you to pursue your dream and how did they help you?

6) What special schools or training did you pursue?

7) What is the most exciting part of what you do?

8) What is the least exciting part of what you do?

9) What are some of the personal benefits of what you do?

10) What are some of the financial rewards of what you do?

11) What are the best schools or training programs in your field?

12) What advice would you give to someone who was just starting out?

13) What books, magazines, or professional organizations would help us learn more about what you do?

14) What is the best book that you've ever read?

15) What was your favorite class in school? Why?

16) Who was your favorite teacher? Why?

Discovery Activities

The following set of activities is designed to help students discover more about themselves. During this process of self discovery, many students will reveal areas of interest that could become their dreams and aspirations. Dreams are born every day during the simplest of activities. A writing activity could reveal a novelist. A speaking activity could reveal a motivational speaker or politician. A dance activity could reveal a professional dancer, gymnast, or athlete. A research activity could reveal a future scientist, researcher, or college professor.

Many things that students like to do are never called dreams. Dreams are typically considered career choices. We generally don't think of a person's desire to golf, fish, ride bicycles, travel, speak foreign languages, cook, dance, sing, paint, draw, etc., as being a dream, or something that they are motivated, intrinsically, to do. The things that we consider to be silly, for many of us, were once our dreams. We just lost them somewhere along the road to reality. The following set of activities is designed to help children explore those things that they like to do, share them with others who have similar interests, write and talk about them to their classmates, and explore more information regarding the full scope of their areas of interest, i.e., professional associations, clubs, books, magazines, etc.

**Fundamental Components of a
Building Dreams School**

The school is student-centered

The dreams and aspirations of the students drive the curriculum and co-curricular activities.

Diversity is acknowledged and validated

Experiences, resources, learning styles, personality types, and giftedness are acknowledged, validated, and utilized throughout the school.

Teams are utilized on various levels

Teacher teams, dream teams, teacher/student morale-building teams, curriculum teams, media center teams, etc., all focused on achieving our vision.

The entire school is a learning center

Resources are constantly being identified, shared, and utilized in achieving our vision.

Activity 49

Dream Portfolio

Objectives

- To help students organize and preserve activities that they are interested in.
- To help students organize and maintain information gathered during the school year that pertains to their dreams and aspirations.
- To help students remain focused on their dreams and aspirations and the work habits, character values, academic activities, and behaviors that are consistent with achieving those dreams and aspirations.

Materials

- Construction paper.
- Newspapers/magazines.
- Book covers.
- Glue.
- Scissors.

The Dream Portfolio may become the most valuable portfolio for your students. In constructing it, they will focus consciously on their dreams and aspirations; what their dream house might look like; what stages of growth and development they will have to go through to achieve their dreams and aspirations (e.g., graduation, marriage, careers, etc.); what character words will describe them; what places they may like to go, foods they may like to eat, languages they may like to speak.

The dream portfolio will not only provide a powerful visual aide of their dreams and aspirations but will represent the place where all of their research papers, special assignments, notes from guest speakers, letters from pen pals, newspaper/magazine articles, photos, etc., will be maintained and stored.

As students work on classroom assignments throughout the year, they will be able to refer to their portfolios for information. They will begin to develop good habits of looking for, cutting out, and saving articles and information relating to their plans for achieving their goals.

The Dream Portfolio will further provide your students with a visual measurement of the activities and work that they are involved in that is consistent with achieving the dreams and aspirations that they have articulated.

Our students are guided by teachers in researching, analyzing, discussing, and developing the real world elements of our micro society: banking; courts; housing; trade and commerce; and local government. Our students went down to a local bank and worked with bank employees in developing their charter. They went down to the City Hall and sat in on City Council and School Board Meetings to develop our City Charter. They designed their currency and developed Trade Days.

We noticed our eighth graders developing a heightened interest in learning. They became concerned with "what and why" they were learning. They began to communicate to our teachers additional things that they wanted to learn.

— Steve Gering, former Principal of West Middle School, Kansas City, Kansas

Procedure:

1) Have students research newspapers, magazines, and books for information that relates to their dreams and aspirations.

For example:

Changes they would like to see in the world.

Places they would like to live.

What their dream house, bedroom, or dining room might look like.

Types of car, clothes, or possessions they dream of having.

Character words that could be used to describe them.

Changes that they would like to see in their communities or in the environment.

Foods that they would like to eat or restaurants where they would like to go.

Books that they would like to read, write, or illustrate.

Careers that they aspire to enter.

The level of college that they would like to complete.

2) Have students cut out articles, pictures, words, etc.

3) Have students copy quotes from books or gather restaurant menus.

4) Have students lay a poster board oblong.

5) Have students draw, write, or create a glue and glitter design of what they dream of becoming or doing on one board.

6) Have students lay out their words, pictures, articles, etc., on both boards.

7) Have students glue their words, pictures, articles, etc., onto one side of the boards only.

8) Have students place the boards together with the completed sides facing outward and staple them together at each end and along the bottom to create an open envelope.

9) Have students enclose a copy of each of the following Dream Sheets in their portfolios.

Books that I've read related to my dreams and aspirations

1. Date _____ Title _____

   Author _____

2. Date _____ Title _____

   Author _____

3. Date _____ Title _____

   Author _____

4. Date _____ Title _____

   Author _____

5. Date _____ Title _____

   Author _____

6. Date _____ Title _____

   Author _____

7. Date _____ Title _____

   Author _____

8. Date _____ Title _____

   Author _____

9. Date _____ Title _____

   Author _____

10. Date _____ Title _____

    Author _____

11. Date _____ Title _____

    Author _____

12. Date _____ Title _____

    Author _____

© Rising Sun Publishing • (800) 524-2813

Wynn/Blassie • © 1995 Rising Sun Publishing • (800) 524-2813
Building Dreams: Elementary School Edition Teacher's Guide

Speakers whom I've heard related to my dreams and aspirations

Date _____ Speaker's Name _____

Occupation _____

Address _____

_____

_____

Telephone Number (_____) _____

Date _____ Speaker's Name _____

Occupation _____

Address _____

_____

_____

Telephone Number (_____) _____

Date _____ Speaker's Name _____

Occupation _____

Address _____

_____

_____

Telephone Number (_____) _____

Date _____ Speaker's Name _____

Occupation _____

Address _____

_____

_____

Telephone Number (_____) _____

© Rising Sun Publishing • (800) 524-2813

Places that I've gone related to my dreams and aspirations

Date _____ Place _____

People that I met and things that I learned: _____

_____

_____

_____

_____

Date _____ Place _____

People that I met and things that I learned: _____

_____

_____

_____

_____

Date _____ Place _____

People that I met and things that I learned: _____

_____

_____

_____

_____

Date _____ Place _____

People that I met and things that I learned: _____

_____

_____

_____

_____

© Rising Sun Publishing • (800) 524-2813

Wynn/Blassie • © 1995 Rising Sun Publishing • (800) 524-2813
Building Dreams: Elementary School Edition Teacher's Guide

People who can help me to achieve my dreams and aspirations

Name _____

Occupation _____

Address _____

_____

_____

Telephone Number (_____) _____

How they can help me: _____

_____

Name _____

Occupation _____

Address _____

_____

_____

Telephone Number (_____) _____

How they can help me: _____

_____

Name _____

Occupation _____

Address _____

_____

_____

Telephone Number (_____) _____

How they can help me: _____

_____

© *Rising Sun Publishing • (800) 524-2813*

Skills that I'm developing that will help me to achieve my dreams and aspirations

Skill or ability: _____

How I will use it: _____

_____

Skill or ability: _____

How I will use it: _____

_____

Skill or ability: _____

How I will use it: _____

_____

Skill or ability: _____

How I will use it: _____

_____

Skill or ability: _____

How I will use it: _____

_____

Skill or ability: _____

How I will use it: _____

_____

Skill or ability: _____

How I will use it: _____

_____

Skill or ability: _____

How I will use it: _____

_____

© Rising Sun Publishing • (800) 524-2813

Wynn/Blassie • © 1995 Rising Sun Publishing • (800) 524-2813
Building Dreams: Elementary School Edition Teacher's Guide

I Dream of Becoming a Paleontologist

Joshua Wade had the dream of becoming a paleontologist. Joshua was acknowledged by his mother to have a great deal of difficulty with writing assignments. Joshua found that gathering and writing his thoughts was a difficult and frustrating process. Despite his struggles, Joshua was inspired and excited about working on a research project regarding *his* dream which lead to the following report:

> My dream is to become a paleontologist. I have always been fascinated by dinosaurs and I enjoy working outdoors. This career would give me the opportunity to travel and the challenge of discovering prehistoric plant and animal life.
>
> To begin this dream, I am going to join a rock and mineral club and go on field trips to fossil digs. After I graduate from high school, I plan to attend the University of Kansas to earn my bachelor's degree, master's degree, and Ph.D. in geology.
>
> I interviewed Mary Blythe, Science Facilitator, whose hobby is paleontology. She encouraged me to pursue this career because of all the new discoveries. She also told me about the primitive working conditions. I will have to endure rain, sun and heat. The work is tedious but Mrs. Blythe said it is all worth it when you make a new discovery.
>
> Paleontology is a hobby I can start now and turn into a career. The experience I gain with rock and mineral clubs can help me in earth science classes during middle school and high school. After I earn my degrees from KU, I would like to get a job with a research team and discover my own dinosaur "Wadeosaurus."
>
> As I gain more experience, I would like to get a job with the Federal Government or an American firm overseas. I would like to participate in research digs in remote field sites. I think it would be exciting to travel to other countries and other areas that have not been researched.
>
> With hard work and dedication, I can earn a scholarship to finance my college education. Research digs are very expensive, but as more new discoveries are made, more money will be available through federal grants. Industry funding is also available to experienced research teams.

In Joshua's interview with the Science Facilitator whose hobby was paleontology, he prepared a list of insightful and well thought-out questions:

> *What are the best things about your hobby?*
> *What are the worst things?*
> *What are important characteristics for a person interested in paleontology?*
> *What should I be doing now to help me get into this field?*
> *What are some of the hurdles I may encounter?*
> *What is the career outlook for paleontology?*
> *What are some of the duties of a paleontologist?*
> *What are the working conditions like?*

Joshua's research and analysis of his dream accumulated such background information as:

Nature of the Work:

Paleontologists study fossils found in geological formations to trace the evolution of plant and animal life and the geological history of the earth.

Working Conditions:

Paleontologist divide their time between field work and office or laboratory work. They often travel to remote field sites by helicopter or jeep and cover large areas by foot. They often work overseas or in remote areas.

Employment:

In 1988, geologists (including paleontologists) held over 42,000 jobs. In addition, about 8,500 persons held such faculty positions in colleges and universities. The federal government employed about 6,500 geologists in 1988. Three-fifth worked for the Department of Interior, some worked for the Departments of Defense, Agriculture, and Commerce; others worked for state agencies. Geologists also worked for non-profit research institutions. Some were employed by American firms overseas.

Training, Qualifications and Advancement:

A bachelor's degree in geology is adequate for entry-level jobs. Better jobs with good advancement require at least a master's degree in geology or geophysics. A Ph.D. is essential for most research positions. Over 500 colleges and universities offer a bachelor's degree in geology and geophysics. Paleontologists need to be able to work as part of a team. They should be curious, analytical, and able to communicate effectively. Those involved with field work must have physical stamina. Paleontologists usually begin their careers in field exploration or as research assistants in laboratories. They are given more difficult assignments as they gain experience.

Job Outlook:

Employment is expected to grow about as fast as the average for all occupations through the year 2000. Paleontologists should have excellent employment opportunities because many experienced paleontologists have left the occupation.

Earnings:

Graduates with a bachelor's degree received an average starting offer of $21,200 per year in 1988. The average salary for geologists in the federal government was about $40,200 to $43,900 per year.

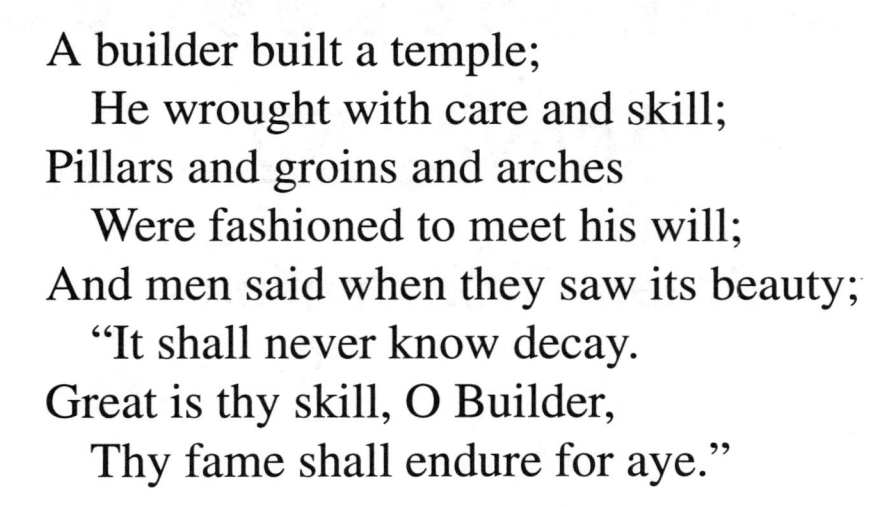

A builder built a temple;
   He wrought with care and skill;
Pillars and groins and arches
   Were fashioned to meet his will;
And men said when they saw its beauty;
   "It shall never know decay.
Great is thy skill, O Builder,
   Thy fame shall endure for aye."

A teacher built a temple;
   She wrought with skill and care;
Forming each pillar with patience,
   Laying each stone with prayer.
None saw the unceasing effort;
   None knew of the marvelous plan;
For the temple the teacher built
   Was unseen by the eyes of man.

Gone is the builder's temple;
   Crumbled into the dust,
Pillar and groin and arches
   Food for consuming rust;
But the temple the teacher built
   Shall endure while the ages roll;
For that beautiful, unseen temple
   Was a child's immortal soul.

                    – Anonymous

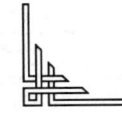

Activity 50

Dream Presentations

Objectives

- To help students internalize what they've learned and how they will apply it.

- To provide students an opportunity to prepare written assignments and oral presentations on what they've learned.

- To help raise individual student self esteem by supporting their efforts toward acquired learning.

Materials

- None required.

The Dream Presentations allow students to internalize what they've learned and how they can apply it. By raising the question, "How can I apply what I've learned toward achieving by dreams and aspirations?", we engage students in higher-order thinking and reasoning. Students begin to internalize the relevance of education toward achieving their future goals.

This activity also allows students an opportunity to re-focus on their dreams and aspirations in a supportive, non-threatening, and encouraging environment.

Procedure:

1) At the end of each grading period, have students write a paper on what they've learned and how will it help them to achieve their dreams and aspirations.

2) Have students prepare an oral presentation to be given before the classroom audience.

3) Have students place their papers into their Dream Portfolios.

For some years, I personally have taught a class called "Prepping for Power." My third-, fourth-, and fifth-grade students learned the tragedy of the seven deadly sins inherent in *Macbeth*. We learned of the indecisiveness of Hamlet from Shakespeare's play, *Hamlet*. We learned that there is no greed like the greed of thinking that something is free. From The *Iliad,* we learned how the Greeks thought that a "freebie" would surely fool the Trojans, and it did. . . We learned the lessons of Machiavelli in the fourth grade. We realize that power seldom gives in to the lower masses. We learned from Voltaire's *Candide* that if we want the best of all worlds, we must be willing to pay the price. In other words, we learned from almost every classic the meaning of hard work, determination, sense of purpose and most of all we learned, "There are no free rides in the world."

— Marva Collins, *Ordinary Children, Extraordinary Teachers*

Developing Dream Teams

Dream teams are special interest groups, special focus clubs, or other actualizing organizations for children that allow them opportunities to increase their skills development as they further explore their special areas of interest. Dream Teams can be developed for students who have both gifts and interests in a broad range of areas such as:

Art/Illustration	Writing	Science
Mathematics	Teaching	Sports
Entrepreneurship	Legal Eagles	Music
Politics	Performing Arts	Radio/Broadcast
Professional Speaking	Book Clubs	Paleontologist
Computer Programming	Franchises	Martial Arts
Community Service	History	Archaeologist
Archeologist	Community Service	Doctor
Coaching	Physicist	Investor
Shakespearean Theatre	Gymnastics	Chef
Translating	International Trade	Ambassador
International Travel	Astronaut	Aviation
Construction	Architect	Sales/Marketing
Sports Card Collecting	Comic Book Collecting	Environmentalist
Law Enforcement	Banking	Swimmer
Model Building	Farming	Chess Player

Dream Teams simply represent the areas of interests of your student population. Areas where your students indicate a willingness to participate and a desire to extend their learning.

Each special interest club will require an academic advisor and will actively search for a mentor.

Activity 51

City Government

Objectives

- To teach students how local government works.
- To provide students with practical experiences in the local legislative process.
- To teach students how to utilize the legislative and local administrative process to achieve their dreams and aspirations that are related to changes in their local communities.

Materials

- None required.

We would like to thank Wanda Hitchye, a third grade teacher at Beaverbrook elementary school in Griffin, Georgia, for implementing such a wonderful activity in her classroom. West Middle School in Kansas City, Kansas, has incorporated a more extensive program where they have created a micro society for their eight grade students where they perform all of the complex tasks of running a city. The elementary school activity focuses primarily on city government and city services.

"Class, we are going to structure a city government in our classroom to help us learn more about how our city works, how and whom makes decisions that affect our schools and communities, how the legislative and criminal justice processes work, and who is responsible for providing services like picking up dead animals from the streets, picking up broken down automobiles, cleaning up graffiti from city property, and deciding whether to place stop signs or traffic lights at intersections."

"We're going to begin by creating a City Charter for our classroom. In our Charter, we're going to decide the responsibilities of our mayor, city council, police commissioner, judge, and conflict mediator."

Procedure:

1) Get a copy of your local City Charter.

2) Facilitate several discussions with students about the major responsibilities or issues in your classroom, e.g., mediating conflicts, enforcing procedures, and your classroom code of conduct, collecting papers, facilitating discussions, etc. You may even associate the responsibilities of the classroom ambassador, teacher's assistant, etc., with positions in city government.

3) Create a City Charter for your classroom and identify students to accept the roles of mayor, city council, police commissioner, conflict mediator, judge, and law enforcement officer.

4) Allow each group of students to perform their responsibilities for the length of a grading period.

5) Use your classroom procedures as your first laws.

6) Create a bulletin board and call it, "I Have A Problem!" Allow students to post real problems such as dead animal removal, needed traffic signals, etc., in their communities that the class can research and identify real solutions to. On-going research can be incorporated into your City Charter.

Activity 52

Models Alert

Objectives

- To teach students good personal hygiene, posture, and etiquette.
- To increase student self esteem.
- To teach students the proper way to eat and conduct themselves in a restaurant.

Materials

- None required.

"We have a program called 'Models Alert' that will be open to the first 25 students who bring back their signed parental consent forms to school. The students involved in the program will meet once a week after school on Wednesdays. Each week, we will have a speaker who will share with us such things as . . ."

As always I was dreaming of ways to promote self esteem in our fifth graders who were about to make a big transition to middle school. Two teachers, Jeanine Cudd and Terri Moore, shared this idea with me. With their strong input and permission from my principal and assistant principal I was on my way to success.

Donna Pelikan and Laqueta Barstow assisted me by working with the 27 students eager to participate in our weekly class. The extraordinary affect of the activity on the students was articulated by Linda Nolan, a summer school teacher, as she shared an encounter with one of the students with me.

Her classroom was discussing France and Bastille Day. During the discussion, they were identifying things associated with France like brie, escargot, wine, and beignets. When I mentioned French bread, one of the students became really excited as she exclaimed, "I know what that is." She was eager to share how she had learned about French bread through the dining experience she'd had with Mrs. Blassie. Mrs. Nolan indicated that the student was very excited about sharing her wonderful and unique experience. She went on to describe what they did, where they went, how they ordered, and what they ate. The student went on to talk about how she will never forget this wonderful experience. I took her to dinner on November 2, 1994, and she was still talking about it in July, 1995!

I implemented the Models Alert Program to build self esteem in fifth graders. Students are able to prepare for achieving their dreams better by increasing their self awareness and by developing desirable personal etiquette.

Procedure:

1) Identify guest speakers and schedule one during each week of the program.

2) Identify several local restaurants that are accessible to your students and send them a letter (see sample letter).

3) Schedule dinner at a restaurant and notify parents about the cost.

4) Coordinate a fashion show committee to help facilitate a fashion show for the participants.

5) Participants may only wear clothes that they already own. Schedule sessions to demonstrate to students how to accessorize what they already have.

6) Demonstrate to students how to write a thank you letter to each guest speaker, the restaurant owner, and any one else who assists with the Models Alert Program.

Sample letter to Restaurant

Dear _____:

There is a group of students at our school who are part of a program where they are learning grooming, personal hygiene, posture, and how to properly conduct themselves in fine restaurants such as yours.

We cannot afford the standard prices of a fine restaurant, so we would like to request that you allow us to dine at your restaurant, with chaperones of course, at a discounted rate to make it affordable for all of the students in our program. The students and chaperones would total approximately _____ people.

If you are able to accommodate our request, please indicate what the discount would be from your normal menu prices. Thereby each of our students would be prepared to pay the appropriate amount, plus tax, and gratuity.

If you are unable to honor our request, we would still like to receive one of your menus because we are collecting menus from the finest restaurants in town to practice ordering skills, paying the check, and computing the gratuity.

We anxiously await your response.

Sincerely,

Models.

Opportunities to grow.

Dining out.

Etiquette.

Lovers of fashion.

Success.

Course Manager: _____

Activity 53

Aspiring Artists Club

Objectives

- To engage students in extensive art instruction.
- To allow personal fulfillment from professional presentation of art work.
- To engage students in the research of careers and opportunities in the various visual mediums.

Materials

- Art materials and supplies.

In many elementary schools, art instruction is presented as little as one day per week for one class period. Students may engage in other artistic activities, periodically, in the classroom; however, gifted or aspiring artists have little opportunity to seriously pursue opportunities in this area.

During his first grade year at Mt. Bethel Elementary School in Marietta, Georgia, my six-year-old son demonstrated a desire to pursue art and illustration. He didn't come home from school proclaiming, "I have a dream to become an artist!" He did what most other children do; he demonstrated a willingness to remain on task for hours while sitting in his room making pencil and pen drawings. His illustrations began appearing everywhere: on paper bags, on napkins, on toilet paper, on his lunch box, etc. The issue was not whether his drawings were that good, only that he had an area of interest that he was motivated, intrinsically, to pursue. He wasn't doing it for grades, affection, recognition, or financial gain. He was doing it because he enjoyed it and he wanted to get better at it. The seeds of a dream had been planted.

"Mychal-David would you like to become an artist?"

"I don't know, dad, I think I still want to race motorcycles."

"Well, Mychal-David, you could still do that, but have you ever thought about drawing pictures like the ones in your books?"

"You mean that I could be a drawer?"

"They're called illustrators. Maybe you and I could even collaborate on a book."

"Col-lab-o-rate?"

"Yes, Mychal-David, that means that we would work together on publishing a book. I could write the book and you could do the illustrations."

"Okay dad, lets collaborate!"

Following that dialogue, my wife and I filled Mychal-David's holiday with art-related gifts, i.e., an easel, apron, paints, cartoon illustration videotapes, pencils, etc. We enrolled our son in after-school art classes offered by our county public schools. We also enrolled him in an art camp during the summer before he entered second grade. We are discussing ideas for a book (our collaborative project) that will hopefully be published during his second grade year.

"We have a program called Aspiring Artists Club that will be open to students who are interested in working on after-school art activities throughout the school year. Anyone who is interested must bring a signed parental consent form back to school. The students involved in the program will meet each day during the after school program. During the school year, we will invite guest speakers who will share with us such things as: painting, drawing, framing, sculpture, and illustrating."

Procedure:

1) Invite guest speakers and schedule them throughout the school year.

2) Have students work more extensively on the curriculum areas of art instruction for the entire week for that curriculum activity.

3) One of the first activities should be to create a portfolio, folder, or box for saving the artwork.

4) Schedule a series of displays or art shows throughout the school year.

5) Schedule field trips to various types of art venues, e.g., art museum, silk screening company, art show, art gallery, greeting card company, computer graphics design company, banner manufacturer, etc.

6) Engage students in hands-on activities leading to experiences such as: designing the school's t-shirt, developing posters and banners, sculptures, masks, etc.

7) Have a year-end art show and reception where students can sell their work, receive awards for their participation, meet professional artists, introduce mentors to their parents, etc. Be sure to professionally present their work via framing, easels, etc.

8) Engage students in reading and research activities about art and the business of art. Students should research art schools, museums, scholarships, grants, etc.

9) Expose students to the multitude of artistic mediums, career opportunities, practicing professionals, and allow them to choose the areas that most interest them.

10) Use the Aspiring Artists Club to decorate the school throughout the school year and to facilitate the creation of various classroom bulletin boards.

In many schools, "art" is taught by a kind of circuit-riding "art teacher," who manages about half an hour a week in any given class. I marvel at such an operation. What is it suppose to accomplish other than to allow the school to claim an "art program?" Let the school system use its funds more wisely by providing in full measure the materials for art needed by the child and by hanging real art shows under the direction of a real artist. Let the children see lots of good art and produce as much art as they wish to produce. The classroom teacher can pose problems and ask questions that will help the child move from discovery to discovery.

— Henry F. Beechhold, *The Creative Classroom*

Sample letter to Professionals

Dear _____:

    We have a group of students at our school who are part of a program called the Aspiring Artists Club. They have been experimenting with different medium and will be doing more extensive work that parallels our curriculum instruction throughout the school year.

    We would appreciate hearing from a professional like you who could share with us your unique insight.

    We are also looking for mentors who can guide students on a continual basis throughout the school year. This could mean as little as one visit per month to our class.

    Some of the topics that our students are interested in learning more about are:

- *T-shirt art and air brushing*
- *Fine art originals and reproductions*
- *Caricature drawings and cartoon illustrations*
- *Computer Graphics*
- *Greeting Cards*
- *Sculpture*
- *Framing and professional presentations*
- *Book illustrations*
- *The manufacturing and reproduction process*

We eagerly anticipate any information you can share with us.

Sincerely,

Sample letter to Parents

Dear Parent,

Thomas Armstrong, in *Awakening Your Child's Natural Genius*, notes:

> For violin great Yehudi Menuhin, the crystallizing experience came when his parents took him to see the San Francisco Symphony Orchestra as a three-year-old. This experience so enthralled him that he asked to be given a violin as well as lessons with the orchestra's principal violinist. His parents provided both. In Albert Einstein's case, the turning point was when his father presented him with a simple scientific instrument that evoked his curiosity. "A wonder of such nature I experienced as a child of 4 or 5 when my father showed me a compass," recalled Einstein. "That this needle behaved in such a determined way did not at all fit into the nature of events. . . I can still remember—or at least believe I can remember—that this experience made a deep and lasting impression upon me."
>
> In each instance, family members provided simple resources, seemingly innocent in themselves, that had a powerful emotional impact upon these creative individuals, pulling them along a path of development that ultimately led to their major life accomplishments.

Each year we have students like the young Pablo Picasso or Michelangelo who are interested in learning more about art than we have time to cover in art classes. For those students, we are creating the Aspiring Artists Club. Students in the club will work on extensive art activities, listen to guest speakers, and do research about art and the business of art.

If your child is interested in joining the *Aspiring Artists Club,* complete the attached permission slip, which also outlines the costs of materials, and return it to school by: _____.

Sincerely,

Activity 54

Aspiring Writers Club

Objectives

- To engage students in more extensive writing instruction.

- To allow personal fulfillment from professional presentation of writing.

- To engage students in researching careers and opportunities in the various areas of writing.

- To help students research and understand book publishing and the book publishing industry.

Materials

- Construction paper.
- Book cover samples.

I would like to thank Sharon Gathers, level 4/5 teacher; Joann Berry, a seventh grade language arts teacher; and Rebecca Zeigler, a level 3/4 teacher from the Felton Laboratory School in Orangeburg, South Carolina, for sharing this activity.

"Class, we are going to create an Aspiring Writers Club for those students who may be interested in seriously pursuing writing and book publishing. We are going to expand what we are learning in class to gain more experience in the real world of writing and book publishing. Some of us may recite poetry, write novels, publish short stories, market, and distribute books or become book editors or reviewers."

Procedure:

1) Form a club based on student interests in writing and book publishing.

2) Discuss, demonstrate, and illustrate various forms of writing, speaking, poetry recital, and storytelling.

3) Research the book-publishing process including the complete spectrum of computer books, copied books, to professionally perfect bound or hard copy books.

4) Research the professional associations for writers, publishers, and other professionals associated with the publishing industry, e.g., publicists, speaker associations, etc.

5) Have students create a chart illustrating the book publishing process with the associated areas of responsibilities, e.g., writer, editor, marketing manager, retail store, distributor, copyright attorney, etc.

6) Collect books, book covers, author's photos, advertising displays, book reviews, etc.

7) Have students experiment with various medium, i.e., greeting cards, posters, plaques, buttons, book markers, etc.

8) Gather samples of various printed products.

9) Break students into smaller groups based on areas of interest, i.e., poetry, fiction, non-fiction, text books, greeting cards, song writing, etc.

10) Provide students with actualizing experiences, e.g., creating holiday greeting cards, school posters, silk screening, buttons, books, book markers, etc.

11) Facilitate some celebratory days for students to display, sell, recite, discuss, and autograph their work.

12) Invite guest speakers who are experienced in the various areas of student interests.

Sample letter to Professionals

Dear _____:

We have a group of students at our school who are part of a program called the Aspiring Writers Club. They have been experimenting with different forms of writing, marketing, book publishing, poetry reading, and storytelling, and will be doing more extensive work that parallels our curriculum instruction throughout the school year.

We would appreciate hearing from a professional like you who could share with us your unique insight.

We are also looking for mentors who can guide students on a continual basis throughout the school year. This could mean as little as one visit per month to our class.

As mentioned above, some of the areas that our students are interested in learning more about are:

— *Poetry writing and reciting*

— *Writing and publishing novels and presenting book reviews*

— *Getting published and self publishing*

— *The responsibilities of people in the publishing industry (e.g., writers, editors, publishers, publicists, distributors, retailers, etc.)*

— *Writing and publishing greeting cards*

— *Song and script writing*

We eagerly anticipate any information you can share with us.

Sincerely,

Sample letter to Parents

Dear Parent,

We do extensive work in language development and writing in school. However, some of our students want to take what they're learning and explore the world of book writing and publishing. Some students want to explore writing verses in greeting cards, songs, and movie scripts. For those students who have an interest in pursuing the business of writing or in simply further developing their own writing, we are creating the Aspiring Writers Club. Students in the club will work on more extensive writing activities, listen to guest speakers, and do research about writing and and the business of publishing.

If your child is interested in joining the *Aspiring Writers Club,* complete the attached permission slip, which also outlines the costs of materials, and return it to school by: _____.

Sincerely,

Activity 55

Radio/Television Broadcast Club

Objectives

- To engage students in more extensive writing and presentation activities.

- To allow students personal fulfillment from the professional presentation of their writing, interviewing, and program development.

- To engage students in the researching careers and opportunities in the various areas of television, radio, and broadcast.

- To help students develop and actualize projects such as: school paper, radio shows, or video tapes of school activities.

Materials

- Appropriate audio and visual equipment.

I would like to thank Donna Holman, level 6-8 foreign languages teacher from the Felton Laboratory School, for sharing this activity.

Donna facilitated a radio show which engaged students in creating and presenting a radio news and talk format at Felton which was recorded and broadcasted on the South Carolina State radio station. Students wrote descriptive papers in conjunction with the publications group and eighth grade students. These papers described the student in his/her own words and the dreams the student wanted to realize and why he/she had chosen them based on his/her personality, strengths, and abilities or interests.

The activity culminated in several 30 minute radio shows where eighth grade students were showcased to the listening audience as people on their way to success with a clear purpose and direction.

Donna observed that this activity allowed students to reflect on their lives. It made them very excited to share their dreams and they seemed to elicit a sense of enthusiasm and importance as a special member in the group and in eventually the world.

A broadcast or video production club can also be utilized to shoot videotapes, record audio tapes, and utilize computer technology for capturing what the school is doing with the dream-building activities. Lessons can be recorded to provide training videotapes. School programs can be videotaped. Students can seek professional mentors at local television and radio stations. Students can engage in writing scripts, interviewing, shooting, editing, production, and distribution of the positive things that are being done at your school. Students will gain hands-on, highly-marketable skills that may, in fact, lead to careers in radio/television broadcasting, writing, acting, and production.

The Radio/Broadcast Club could easily become the most powerful and engaging club at a school. Think about the possibilities of engaging students in writing, acting in, producing, marketing, and distributing school-generated interview videotapes, music videotapes, training videotapes, etc. The opportunities are as great as you and your students' imaginations. If there is any dream team that all schools should have, this is it!

Sample letter to Professionals

Dear _____:

We have a group of students at our school who are part of a program called the Radio/Television Broadcast Club. They will be engaging in many aspects of audio and video tape production in such areas as: conceptualizing, writing, interviewing, acting, and producing.

We would appreciate hearing from a professional like you who could share with us your unique insight.

We are also looking for opportunities to visit radio/television stations and production studios; meetings with station managers, program directors, and personalities to provide our students with as much exposure as possible to the creative energies and business of professional media. We are also interested in mentors who can guide students on a continual basis throughout the school year. This could mean as little as one visit per month to our class.

As mentioned above, some of the areas that our students are interested in learning more about are:

— *All aspects of writing, preparing, and producing shows*

— *Professional tips on interviewing and promotions*

— *Professional tips on pre- and post-production*

We eagerly anticipate any information you can share with us.

Sincerely,

Activity 56

Guest Speakers

Objectives

- To prepare students for gathering information and asking questions of experts in their respective areas of interest.

- To help students acquire skills at asking questions, reviewing information, and dialoguing about what they've learn.

Materials

- None required.

"Class, we have a schedule of guest speakers coming into our classroom this year. Most of our guest speakers are living the dreams that many of you have. Since our guest speakers are experts at what they do, we want to take advantage of this unique opportunity by deciding what we would like for them to discuss and what types of questions we want to ask our guest speakers. After our guest speakers leave, we are going to review what we have learned and write them a thank-you note for coming to our class."

Guest speakers can make a powerful impact upon students. They can also provide a rare opportunity for students to meet, greet, and ask questions of someone who may be living their dream. Guest speakers also offer extraordinary instructional opportunities. Students are introduced to varied areas of interests, individual struggles, how people overcome hardships and challenges, and how expertise and individual skills can be applied.

Pre-activity:

1) Ask for a photograph, biography, and any other information that your guest speaker can provide at least a week before his/her coming. Ask the guest speaker for permission to tape the presentation.

2) Prepare a GUEST SPEAKER bulletin board and post the information regarding your guest speaker so that your classroom can read about the speaker before the visit. This also gives your guest speaker celebrity status.

3) "Class, our guest speaker will be Mr. Jones, an entrepreneur. Mr. Jones owns his own automobile repair shop. Many of you have dreams of becoming an entrepreneur. What are some of the questions that we will want to ask Mr. Jones?"

Write the questions on the board so that your students may copy them. Pass out copies of the Speaker Questionnaire on the following page to help your students focus on additional questions.

Procedures for welcoming and thanking your guest speakers:

1) Have a designated student greet the guest speaker (classroom ambassador or a student who aspires toward the career of the guest speaker).
2) Have your classroom recite your Welcome.
3) Have students put their current work away and prepare themselves to:
   - Listen
   - Take notes
   - Ask questions
4) Have students prepare and place name cards on their desks.
5) Prepare either a video tape or audio tape of the guest speaker to go into your speaker's library.
6) Keep track of the time to ensure that there is time for questions.
7) At the conclusion of the presentation and after all questions have been asked, have a designated student thank the presenter and present a special gift.
8) The class should applaud after the presentation.
9) Take a picture of the guest speaker with the student representative responsible for greeting the guest speaker.

Post-activity:

1) "Write a paper about what you learned from our guest speaker."
2) Use the speaker questionnaire as the basis for the classroom discussion to recall facts about the speaker and the information presented.

   "Without referring to your notes, let's see how much we can recall from what our speaker talked about."
3) Select a paper to post on your "Guest Speaker Wall of Fame."
4) Post the picture of the guest speaker next to the student paper.

Middle school students share their dreams with elementary school students.

Date _____ Speaker's Name _____

Address _____

_____

Telephone (_____) _____

How old were you when you first decided to pursue this dream? _____

_____

_____

What were some of the challenges and obstacles that you had to overcome?

_____

_____

_____

Who were the most influential people in your life in helping you to pursue your dreams and how did they help you?

_____

_____

What special schools or training do you need? _____

_____

_____

_____

_____

What is the most exciting part of what you do? _____

_____

_____

What is the least exciting part of what you do? _____

_____

_____

What are some of the personal benefits in what you do?

_____
_____
_____
_____
_____

What are some of the financial rewards in what you do?

_____
_____
_____
_____
_____

What are the best schools or training programs in your field?

_____
_____
_____

What advice would you give to someone who was just starting out? What books, magazines, or professional organizations would help us learn more about what you do?

_____
_____
_____
_____
_____

Things to say to encourage a child

Say: You're incredible.
Don't say: What's wrong with you?
Say: Hold that thought so that we can discuss it later.
Don't say: Shut up.
Say: That's an innovative and creative way of doing it.
Don't say: That's stupid.
Say: I'm really proud of you when you accept responsibility.
Don't say: Why don't you do your job and stop whining.
Say: Remember to say, "Excuse me."
Don't say: Stop butting in when I'm talking.
Say: You did a wonderful job, you'll going to become a great . . .
Don't say: That's nice.
Say: Explain to me why you did that, it would have never occurred to me to do it that way.
Don't say: Why did you do such a stupid thing?
Say: I'm really proud of the way that you handled that.
Don't say: You'd better had done what I told you.
Say: What type of things would you like to do today?
Don't say: I don't care what you want to do.
Say: I appreciate your thoughts, however we aren't going to discuss this anymore.
Don't say: I don't care what you think.
Say: How do you feel about this?
Don't say: Who cares how you feel.
Say: Can I count on you to help me?
Don't say: You'd better do it, because I said do it!
Say: I'd like to introduce you to my son, he dreams of one day becoming a great . . .
Don't say: Yeah, that's my son, he drives me crazy.
Say: I love you, I'll see you in the morning.
Don't say: Go to bed.
Say: This is great work, will you autograph it for me so that I can frame it?
Don't say: Why didn't you do . . .
Say: "I love you," more than you yell.
Say: "I love you," more than you criticize.

© Mychal Wynn/Rising Sun Publishing (800) 524-2813

Activity 57

Dream Day Activities

Objective

- To provide students with an actualizing experience for applying what they have learned regarding their dreams and aspirations.

Materials

- Various (depending upon level of school involvement).

The Dream Day activities allow students to actualize various dreams and aspirations. The scope of activities can be as simple as dressing as your dream to actually filling the day with student presentations, special events, art shows, book signings, interviews with guest speakers, etc.

Procedure:

1) Contact guest speakers to talk to students regarding their dreams and aspirations.

2) Recognize volunteers, guest speakers, mentors, etc., who have been working with students to help them actualize their dreams and aspirations.

3) Provide opportunities for students to take field trips from the school onto the sites of their dreams and aspirations.

4) Provide special recognition for students who exemplify the hard work, determination, perseverance, and character values in writing papers, working in the capacity of apprenticeships, published books, created art work, participated in performances, competed in formal competitions, or achieved other actualizing experiences during the school year.

5) Provide recognition for teachers who have contributed to students' actualizing their dreams and aspirations.

6) Provide recognition for teachers who have achieved their dreams and aspirations during the school year, e.g., graduate degrees, conferences, papers or books published, grants received, special hobbies or interests in which goals were realized, etc.

Activity 58

Saying "Thank You"

Objectives

- To enhance language and written communications skills.
- To model good citizenship behavior.

Materials

- None required.

"Class I would like for you to think about some of the people who have helped you. I'd like you to write the name of at least one teacher at the school who has helped you in some way toward achieving your dreams and aspirations. I'd also like you to think of another person who has helped you. Perhaps one of our guest speakers, the principal, a counselor, someone in your family, or someone you were introduced to this year who has encouraged and supported you."

Procedure:

1) "Write a letter to one of your teachers telling:"

   A. What he/she did that made you feel good or learn.

   B. How it made you feel.

   C. Thank he/she for supporting you.

2) "Write a letter to a guest speaker, mentor, volunteer, your parent, or anyone who in some way helped or encouraged you toward achieving your dreams and aspirations. Tell them:"

   A. What he/she did and why you appreciate what they did.

   B. How it helped you.

   C. Thank him/her for supporting you.

3) Give the letters to the teachers and mail the letters to those people not at the school site.

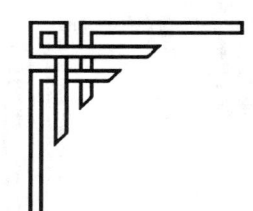

What did I do today?

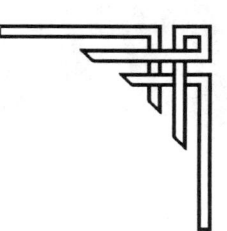

- How many hugs did I give or hands did I shake?

- How many smiles did I give and kind words did I say?

- How many life-affirming dream-building words like wonderful, incredible, fantastic, extraordinary, insightful, thoughtful, or marvelous did I say or write?

- Did I utter such words, declarations, or accusations regarding children as thoughtless, careless, useless, not paying attention, sloppy, silly, or other prophetic declarations of failure?

- Did I smile as much at the "slow" students as I did at the "bright" students?

- Did I have as many kind words and positive compliments for the "dirty" students as I did for the "pretty" students?

- Did I provide as many opportunities for the students "likely to get the answer wrong," as I did for those "likely to get the answer right?"

- Did I affirm the same possibilities of success for the students who came to me today from "challenging" family environments as I did for those who came from "good" families?

- Did I use the same tone of voice and the same language with all of my students regardless of what they looked like, what they smelled like, where they came from, who their parents were, what their IQs were, or what their problems were?

- Did I encourage ALL of my students to dream?

© Mychal Wynn/Rising Sun Publishing (800) 524-2813

Activity 59

Nice Things About You

Objectives

- To provide students with an opportunity to recognize special qualities in each classmate.
- To contribute toward raising student self esteem.
- To acknowledge each student's value to the class.

Materials

- None required.

Procedure:

1) Have each student take a sheet of paper and write the names of all classmates onto the paper, skipping a line between names.

2) Below each name have each student write one comment representing the nicest thing they know about that person.

3) Take each paper and combine the comments into individual papers for each student.

4) Display the papers in the classroom along with a photo of each student for a period of time and then return the materials to your students.

Helping students to appreciate each other builds a brighter future.

Activity 60

Post-Assessment

Objectives

- To survey students' interests in the learning experience of the Dream-Building Program.

- To help students synthesize the knowledge gained from the activities that they've engaged in.

- To allow students an opportunity to evaluate the learning experience along with the teacher's and school's effectiveness in helping them to discover their dreams and aspirations.

Materials

- Student evaluation forms.

Dream-Building Program - Student Survey

1) What were your dreams and aspirations at the beginning of this school year?

___

2) Describe how your dreams and aspirations have changed as a result of this school year.

___

3) Describe how your teacher has been supportive of your dreams and aspirations.

_____
_____
_____
_____
_____
_____
_____
_____
_____
_____
_____

4) Describe how students, counselors, and other people at your school have been supportive of your dreams and aspirations.

_____
_____
_____
_____
_____
_____
_____
_____
_____
_____
_____

5) What type of things did you learn in school this year that will help you to achieve your dreams and aspirations?

_____
_____
_____
_____
_____
_____
_____
_____
_____
_____
_____
_____
_____
_____
_____
_____
_____
_____
_____
_____
_____
_____
_____
_____

6) List some of the books that you read, people you met, speakers you heard, and classroom activities or discussions you participated in that taught you more about how to achieve your dreams and aspirations.

Books: _____
_____
_____
_____
_____
_____

People: _____
_____
_____
_____
_____
_____

Activities/Discussions: _____
_____
_____
_____
_____
_____
_____
_____
_____
_____

7) List the favorite activities that you participated in this year relating to your dreams and aspirations and describe how they helped you.

8) Check <u>each</u> of the following expressions that you agree with:

❐ Students support each other ❐ Students put down each other
❐ Teachers encourage students ❐ Teachers put down students

❐ This school helps students feel good about themselves.
❐ This school doesn't care how students feel about themselves.

❐ Most of my classes relate to my dreams.
❐ Some of my classes relate to my dreams.
❐ None of my classes relate to my dreams.

❐ I learned a lot this year about what I have to do to achieve my dreams.
❐ I learned a little this year about what I have to do to achieve my dreams.
❐ I didn't learn anything this year about what I have to do to achieve my dreams.

❐ My school is helping me to achieve my dreams and aspirations.
❐ My school doesn't care about me or my dreams.

❐ My teacher is helping me to achieve my dreams and aspirations.
❐ My teacher doesn't care about me or my dreams.

❐ I participated on a Dream Team or Special Interest Club.
❐ There were no Dream Teams in my area of interest.

My area of interest is: _____

❐ I wanted to participate on a Dream Team but I couldn't for the following reasons:
_____
_____

❐ I went on Dream-Building Field Trips.
❐ There were no Dream-Building Field Trips at my school.

❐ I heard guest speakers who shared information about how they achieved their dreams.
❐ The Dream-Building Program and activities are important to me.
❐ I don't care about the Dream-Building Program or activities.

❐ Next year I would like to continue the Dream-Building Program and activities.
❐ Next year I am going to a new school.

Appendix

I. Parkway School District's Character Values and Definitions.

II. Eagle Word List and Definitions.

III. Building Dreams Word List and Definitions.

IV. Bibliography.

Parkway School District's Character Values

To achieve these objectives, the Board directs the Superintendent of Schools to establish procedures which ensure that the following core values are infused throughout the environment of the Parkway School District and its curriculum.

<u>Personal Values</u>: Accountability, honesty, integrity, responsibility, self-esteem.

<u>Social Values</u>: Abstinence, caring about others, commitment to family, positive work ethic, respect for others.

<u>Civic Values</u>: Equality, freedom, justice, respect for authority, respect for property.

Definitions

Personal Values

1. Accountability

Accepting the consequences of one's actions as well as the credit or blame for them.

2. Honesty

Being truthful.

3. Integrity

Adherence to truth, that which is right, fair, and honorable, in all dealings.

4. Responsibility

Dependable fulfillment of obligations to one's self and others.

5. Respect for Self

Having and demonstrating a positive belief in one's intrinsic worth.

Social Values

6. Abstinence*

Voluntarily refraining from an improper indulgence in alcohol, drugs, and sex.

7. Caring about others

A sense of responsibility for the well-being of other people.

8. Commitment to family

Being sensitive to, and supportive of, the needs of the family.

9. Positive work ethic

Performing to the best of one's ability.

10. Respect for others

To show consideration, appreciation, tolerance and good manners toward other people.

*Abstinence, in this context, refers specifically to alcohol, drugs, and sex. For our students, this is, to a great extent, defined by the law. In the case of adults, this refers to supporting the concept in school settings. While the district cannot dictate personal standards or private conduct by staff, it must be recognized that there can be occasions, away from the school setting, where one's example would be greatly compromised by inappropriate conduct, and that this could have an effect on a staff member's effectiveness.

Civic Values

11. Equality

All people are entitled to the same rights.

12. Freedom

The right to choose one's words and actions without infringing on the rights of others.

13. Justice

Fair treatment.

14. Respect for authority

Showing consideration and regard for people in positions of responsibility.

15. Respect for property

Showing consideration and regard for public property and things belonging to others.

— Policy adopted by Parkway School District on April 9, 1992.

Eagle Word List and Definitions

awesome

Remarkable; outstanding. Inspiring awe. Expressing awe.

beautiful

Having qualities that delight the senses, especially the sense of sight. Exciting intellectual or emotional admiration.

character

A person's reputation. Moral or ethical strength. The combination of qualities that distinguishes one person, group, or thing from another.

compassion

Deep awareness of the suffering of another coupled with the wish to relieve it.

confidence

Trust or faith in one's self, another person, or something. A feeling of assurance, especially of self-assurance.

considerate

Regard for the needs or feelings of others.

courage

The state or quality of mind or spirit that enables one to face danger, fear, or vicissitudes [unexpected changes encountered in one's life] with bravery, confidence, and resolution.

courteous

Characterized by gracious consideration toward others.

determination

Firmness of purpose; resolve.

dignity

Carrying yourself as though you are worthy of esteem and respect. Demonstrating poise and self-respect.

diligent

To persist or remain constant to a purpose, an idea, or a task in the face of obstacles or discouragement, painstaking effort.

encourage

To inspire with hope, courage, or confidence. To give support to.

excellent

Of the highest or finest quality; exceptionally good of its kind.

extraordinary

Beyond what is ordinary or usual. Highly exceptional; remarkable.

faith

Confident belief in the truth, value, or trustworthiness of a person, an idea, or a thing. Belief that does not rest on logical proof or material evidence. Loyalty to a person or thing; allegiance. A set of principles or beliefs.

fantastic

Wonderful or superb; remarkable.

fortitude

Strength of mind that allows one to endure pain or adversity [hardship, misfortune] with courage.

incredible

So implausible as to elicit disbelief. Astonishing.

inspire

To affect, guide, or arouse by divine influence. To fill with enlivening or exalting emotion. To stimulate to action; motivate. To stimulate energies, ideals, or reverence [showing respect or love].

integrity

Steadfast adherence to a strict moral or ethical code.

intelligence

The capacity to acquire and apply knowledge. The faculty of thought and reason. Superior powers of the mind.

helpful

Providing assistance; useful.

justice

The quality of being just; fairness. The principle of moral rightness; moral rightness in action or attitude; righteousness. The upholding of what is just, especially fair treatment and due reward in accordance with honor, standards, or law. Conformity to truth, fact, or sound reason.

kind

Of a friendly, generous, or warm-hearted nature. Showing sympathy or understanding; charitable. Humane; considerate.

loyal

Steadfast in allegiance, faithful to a person, an ideal, a custom, a cause, or a duty.

magnificent

Grand or noble in thought or deed; exalted. Outstanding of its kind; superlative.

marvelous

Causing wonder or astonishment. Of the highest or best kind or quality; first-rate.

outstanding

Standing out among others of its kind; prominent. Superior; distinguished.

perseverance

Steady persistence in adhering to a course of action, a belief, or a purpose; steadfastness.

persistent

Refusing to give up or let go; persevering obstinately, enduring.

relentless

Unyielding in severity or strictness; unrelenting. Steady and persistent; unremitting.

remarkable

Worthy of notice. Attracting notice as being unusual or extraordinary.

resilient

Marked by the ability to recover readily, as from misfortune.

responsible

Involving personal accountability or ability to act without guidance or superior authority. Able to make moral or rational decisions on one's own and therefore answerable for one's behavior. Able to be trusted or depended upon; reliable.

reverence

A feeling of profound awe and respect and often love. An act showing respect, especially a bow or curtsy.

self-esteem

Pride in oneself; self-respect.

self-respect

Demonstrating respect for yourself through your character and conduct.

strong

Having force of character, will, morality, or intelligence. Having or showing ability or achievement in a specified field. Capable of withstanding force or wear; solid, tough, or firm. Not easily defeated or upset.

stupendous

Of astounding force, volume, degree, or excellence; marvelous.

supportive

Furnishing support or assistance.

tenacious

Holding together firmly or tending to hold persistently to something, such as a point of view.

valiant

Possessing valor; brave. Marked by or done with valor.

wonderful

Capable of eliciting wonder; astonishing. Admirable; excellent.

Definitions taken from the <u>American Heritage Dictionary</u>. Houghton Mifflin Company:1992.

Building Dreams Word List and Definitions

brilliant

Full of light; shining. Glorious; magnificent. Superb; wonderful. Marked by unusual and impressive intelligence.

commitment

To maintain responsibility to do, perform, or perpetrate. To fulfill a trust, charge or responsibility.

compassion

Deep awareness of the suffering of others coupled with the wish to relieve it.

dedicated

To commit (oneself) to a particular course of thought or action.

dependable

Trustworthy. Others are able to place confidence in your commitment and sense of duty.

empowered

To have a sense of personal power and one's ability to confront and overcome obstacles.

ethical

Being in accordance with the accepted principles of right and wrong that govern the conduct of a profession.

fairness

Having or exhibiting a disposition that is free of favoritism or bias; impartial. Consistent with rules, logic, or ethics.

helpful

Providing assistance; useful.

honest

Displaying integrity; upright. Not deceptive or fraudulent; genuine. Equitable; fair. Of good repute; respectable.

motivated

To have the incentive to work toward something.

reliable

Capable of being relied on; dependable.

strength

The state, property, or quality of being strong. The power to resist strain or stress; durability. The ability to maintain a moral or intellectual position firmly. Capacity or potential for effective action.

tenacity

The quality of holding or tending to hold persistently to something, such as a point of view.

trustworthy

Warranting trust; reliable. A person who exhibits honesty.

unyielding

Refusing to give way to pressure, argument, or influence. Remaining determined to continue despite in the face of obstacles.

vision

Unusual competence in perception; intelligent foresight. The ability to develop a mental image produced by the imagination.

Definitions taken from the American Heritage Dictionary. Houghton Mifflin Company:1992.

Bibliography

Armstrong, Thomas. In Their Own Way. New York, NY: Jeremy P. Tarcher, Inc., (1987).

_____. Awakening Your Child's Natural Genius. Los Angeles, CA: Jeremy P. Tarcher, Inc, (1991).

Beechhold, Henry F. The Creative Classroom. New York, NY: Scribner, (1971).

Canfield, Jack, Hansen, Mark Victor. Chicken Soup for the Soul. Deerfield Beach, FL: Health Communications, (1993).

_____. A 2nd Helping of Chicken Soup for the Soul. Deerfield Beach, FL: Health Communications, (1995).

Carson, Ben. Gifted Hands. Washington, DC: Review and Herald Publishing, (1990).

Collins, Marva. Ordinary Children, Extraordinary Teachers. Norfolk, VA: Hampton Roads Publishing, (1992).

Dunn, Rita, Dunn, Kenneth, and Treffinger, Donald. Bringing Out The Giftedness In Your Child. New York, NY: John Wiley & Sons, Inc., (1992).

Edelston, Matin, Buhagiar, Marion. "I" Power. Fort Lee, NJ: Barricade Books, (1992).

Gardner, Howard. Frames of Mind: The Theory of Multiple Intelligences. New York, NY: Harper and Row, (1983).

_____. The Unschooled Mind: How Children Think & How Schools Should Teach. New York:NY: BasicBooks, (1991).

Kohn, Alfie. Punished by Rewards. New York: Houghton Mifflin, (1993).

Myers, Isabel Briggs, Myers, Peter B. Gifts Differing. Palo Alto, CA: Consulting Psychologists, (1980).

Newsweek Magazine. Your Child's Brain and Why Do Schools Flunk Biology? (February 19, 1996).

William Purkey, John Novak. Inviting School Success: A Self-concept Approach to Teaching. By Invitation Only. Phi Delta Kappa, (1988).

Wong, Harry K. , Wong, R.T. The First Days of School. Sunnyvale, CA: Harry K. Wong Publications, (1991)

Wynn, Mychal. Building Dreams: Helping Students Discover Their Potential. Marietta, GA: Rising Sun Publishing, (1996).

_____. Building Dreams: Helping Students Discover Their Potential, Teacher, Parent, Mentor Workbook. Marietta, GA: Rising Sun Publishing, (1994).

_____. Empowering African-American Males to Succeed: A Ten-Step Approach for Parents and Teachers. Marietta, GA: Rising Sun Publishing, (1992).

_____. Don't Quit – Inspirational Poetry. Marietta, GA: Rising Sun Publishing, (1990).

_____. The Eagles who Thought They were Chickens. Marietta, GA: Rising Sun Publishing, (1994).

Photos and other Acknowledgements

Cover photo of Mychal Wynn. Lisa Plasker.
Welborn Elementary School, Kansas City, Kansas.
West Middle School, Kansas City, Kansas.
Fourth Ward Elementary School, Griffin, Georgia.
Los Angeles Unified School District Language Development Program for African American Students.
Carman Trails Elementary School. Manchester, Missouri.
Our Class Pledge. Sharon Moazzen.
Character Values. Parkway School District.
Parent's letter to my child's teacher. Donna Pelikan.
Parent letters. Beth Wendling.
Traffic Light Book. Toni Douglas.
Traffic Light Illustration. Ralph Gray.
Fight Free Bulletin Board. Peggy Dolan.
About Goals. Robin White, a student at West Middle School.
I Dream of Becoming a Paleontologist. Joshua Wade
Character Values. Linda McKay.
Models Alert. Donna Pelikan and Laqueta Barstow.

Share your success!

If you use an activity outlined in this book, send us a photo or write us a letter of what you achieved as a result of the activity; how it affected your students; what types of things you observed in student behavior, interests, participation, and skill level increases.

If you have an activity that you would like to have considered for our forthcoming <u>Building Dreams: Elementary School Activity Book</u>, please forward your activity as outlined in Activity 3, Teacher Idea Board/Activity Book.

Include photos and samples of students' work with your activity. Be sure to include your name, grade level, school, school phone number, FAX number (if available), and your expressed permission for us to reprint your activity.

Send to:

> Rising Sun Publishing/Teacher Activities Desk
> P.O. Box 70906
> Marietta, GA 30007-0906
> or FAX to (770) 587-0862

Please do not call regarding your activity. We evaluate each activity and respond only to those activities that are being considered for inclusion in a forthcoming publication. If you want your materials returned, please include a stamped, self-addressed envelope.

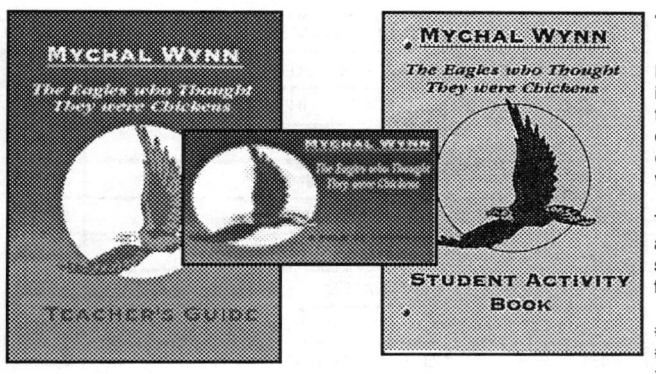

The Eagles who Thought They were Chickens

Mychal takes us on a powerful, spiritual journey as the eagles gain their self esteem and self image when they encounter another eagle who tells them of their culture and heritage. Within their differences is embodied their special gift of flight, their special ability to soar through the clouds. Like the eagles, people are often scorned and ridiculed for being different. This book encourages the celebration of individual uniqueness and the discovery of the brilliance that is within everyone.

The Teacher's Guide and Student Activity Book lead students in grades K-12 through 12 activities that help students internalize the positive, reaffirming language of the eagles, the spirit to take ownership of their individual behavior, the courage to support each other, and the faith to follow their individual dreams and aspirations.

#5601 Book (8 1/2 x 5 1/2, 37 pgs)   ISBN 1-880463-12-1 $4.95
#5602 Teacher's Guide (8 1/2 x 11, 66 pgs) ISBN 1-880463-18-0 $9.95
#5603 Student Activity Book (8 1/2 x 11, 91 pgs) ISBN 1-880463-19-9 $5.95

Building Dreams: Helping Students Discover Their Potential

The Building Dreams program is revolutionizing how we teach, parent, mentor, and counsel children. This holistically integrated program outlines strategies and activities that demonstrate how to bond with children, understand their unique personality types, learning styles, and areas of intrinsic motivation as the road along which we unlock their dreams and aspirations.

The Teacher, Parent, Mentor Workbook outlines how to structure an environment that nurtures the dreams and aspirations of children.

The Elementary School Edition outlines 60 classroom activities that structure a nurturing, non-threatening environment that encourages children to discover their dreams and aspirations; how teachers can become more effective in managing their classrooms; how to reduce conflicts and increase self esteem; how to engage students in continual exploratory activities that increase language, writing, and comprehension skills as they journey toward their dreams and aspirations; how to identify mentors and business partners leading to apprenticeship opportunities; and how to create a dream-building spirit in your school. Full of charts, classroom procedures, learning style and personality type information, sample letters, and classroom activities. Everything you need to turn your classroom into a field of dreams!

#5801 Book (6 x 9)   ISBN 1-880463-12-1 $15.95
#5802 Teacher, Parent, Mentor Workbook (8 1/2 x 11, 125 pgs) ISBN 1-880463-18-0 $ 9.95
#5901 Elementary School Teacher's Guide (8 1/2 x 11, 320 pgs) ISBN 1-880463-19-9 $29.95

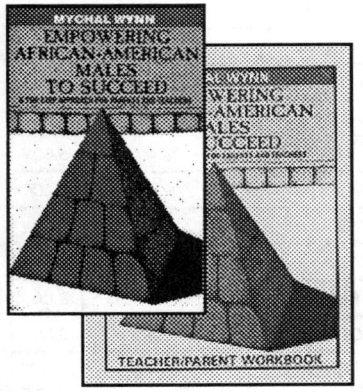

Empowering African-American Males to Succeed: A Ten-Step Approach for Parents and Teachers

Through an enlightening blend of research data and inspirational personal stories the author outlines a ten-step model for helping young African-American males to set goals, visualize achievement, and develop an empowered consciousness. Clear and cohesive strategies and hands-on activities are presented. Exercises are outlined that help parents and teachers better understand, encourage, and motivate African-American young men.

Book (6 x 9, 144 pgs)   ISBN 1-880463-01-6 $15.95
Teacher/parent workbook (8 1/2 x 11, 96 pgs) ISBN 1-880463-02-4 $ 9.95

Don't Quit — Inspirational Poetry

The book that started it all. Mychal Wynn's critically acclaimed book of inspirational poetry containing 26 poems of inspiration and affirmation. Each verse is complimented by a famous quotation which reinforces the spirit of the poem. The verses take the reader on an inspirational journey through personal affirmations of perseverance and determination to confirmation of faith and friendship.

Includes such favorites as *"Born To Win; A Pledge of Friendship; A Pledge to Myself; If You Are My Friend; Be A Winner; and Don't Quit."*

Book (5 1/2 x 8 1/2, 53 pgs)   ISBN 1-880463-26-1 $ 9.95

For ordering information contact:

Rising **S**un **P**ublishing
P.O. Box 70906
Marietta, GA 30007

Phone: (800) 524-2813
FAX: (770) 587-0862

ITEM	BOOKS & POSTERS [** Available as note card]	PRICE
5002	ISBN: 1-880463-26-1 *DON'T QUIT – INSPIRATIONAL POETRY*	9.95
5101	ISBN: 1-880463-01-6 *EMPOWERING AFRICAN-AMERICAN MALES*	15.95
5102	ISBN: 1-880463-02-4 *EMPOWERING AFRI-AMER MALES WRKBK*	9.95
5601	ISBN: 1-880463-12-1 *Eagles who Thought They were Chickens*	4.95
5602	ISBN: 1-880463-18-0 *Eagles Teacher's Guide*	9.95
5603	ISBN: 1-880463-19-9 *Eagles Student Activity Book*	5.95
5701	ISBN: 1-880463-34-2 *ENOUGH IS ENOUGH*	9.95
5800	ISBN: 1-880463-44-X *BUILDING DREAMS, STUDENT LAB*	FALL
5801	ISBN: 1-880463-41-5 *BUILDING DREAMS, BOOK*	15.95
5802	ISBN: 1-880463-42-3 *BUILDING DREAMS, TEACHER WRKBK*	9.95
5901	ISBN: 1-880463-45-8 *Building Dreams: Elem. Schl Tch's Guide*	29.95
8851	ISBN: 09632074-8-2 *The Nubian Student Edition*	21.95
8852	ISBN: 1-886218-01-3 *The Nubian Teacher's Guide*	14.95
8853	ISBN: 09632074-1-5 *The Legend of the Golden Hawk*	4.95
8854	ISBN: 09632074-X-X *Journey to Clay Mountain*	4.95
8855	ISBN: 09632074-3-1 *Lost on Victoria Lake*	4.95
8001	ISBN: 0-87477-608-2 *Awakening Your Child's Natural Genius*	13.95
8101	ISBN: 0-87477-572-8 *Marva Collin's Way*	9.95
8102	ISBN: 1-878901-41-9 *Ordinary Children, Extraordinary Teachers*	12.95
8200	ISBN: 0-932935-39-7 *Seven Ways of Knowing - Multiple Intelligences*	29.95
1	A CREED OF FAITH — UNLAMINATED	2.00
101	A CREED OF FAITH — LAMINATED	3.50
2	A CURIOUS CHILD — UNLAMINATED	2.00
201	A CURIOUS CHILD — LAMINATED	3.50
3	*A MAN IS — UNLAMINATED	2.00
301	A MAN IS — LAMINATED	3.50
4	**A PLEDGE OF FRIENDSHIP — UNLAMINATED	2.00
401	A PLEDGE OF FRIENDSHIP — LAMINATED	3.50
5	**A PLEDGE TO MYSELF — UNLAMINATED	2.00
501	A PLEDGE TO MYSELF — LAMINATED	3.50
7	**ATTITUDE OF CHANCE — UNLAMINATED	2.00
701	ATTITUDE OF CHANCE — LAMINATED	3.50
8	**BE A WINNER — UNLAMINATED	2.00
801	BE A WINNER — LAMINATED	3.50
10	**BE THE CAPTAIN OF YOUR SHIP — UNLAMINATED	2.00
1001	BE THE CAPTAIN OF YOUR SHIP — LAMINATED	3.50
11	**BORN TO WIN — UNLAMINATED	2.00
1101	BORN TO WIN — LAMINATED	3.50
12	CHILDREN WE CARE — UNLAMINATED	2.00
1201	CHILDREN WE CARE — LAMINATED	3.50
13	**DARE — UNLAMINATED	2.00
1301	DARE — LAMINATED	3.50
14	*DIGNITY — UNLAMINATED	2.00
1401	DIGNITY — LAMINATED	3.50
16	**I AM — UNLAMINATED	2.00
1601	I AM — LAMINATED	3.50
15	**DON'T QUIT — UNLAMINATED	2.00
1501	DON'T QUIT — LAMINATED	3.50

17	I AM THE BLACK CHILD — UNLAMINATED	2.00
1701	I AM THE BLACK CHILD — LAMINATED	3.50
18	**IF YOU AND I SHOULD DIFFER — UNLAMINATED	2.00
1801	IF YOU AND I SHOULD DIFFER — LAMINATED	3.50
19	**IF YOU ARE MY FRIEND — UNLAMINATED	2.00
1901	IF YOU ARE MY FRIEND — LAMINATED	3.50
20	**IF WE DO NOT TRY — UNLAMINATED	2.00
2001	IF WE DO NOT TRY — LAMINATED	3.50
21	**LIFE IS OFTEN DIFFICULT — UNLAMINATED	2.00
2101	LIFE IS OFTEN DIFFICULT — LAMINATED	3.50
22	**OVERCOMING DARKNESS — UNLAMINATED	2.00
2201	OVERCOMING DARKNESS — LAMINATED	3.50
23	REMEMBERING FROM WHENCE WE CAME — UNLAMINATED	2.00
2301	REMEMBERING FROM WHENCE WE CAME — LAMINATED	3.50
24	**SUCCESS — UNLAMINATED	2.00
2401	SUCCESS — LAMINATED	3.50
25	**THANK YOU FATHER — UNLAMINATED	2.00
2501	THANK YOU FATHER — LAMINATED	3.50
26	**THE SPIRIT WITHIN YOU — UNLAMINATED	2.00
2601	THE SPIRIT WITHIN YOU — LAMINATED	3.50
27	*THE LEGACY LIVES — UNLAMINATED	2.00
2701	THE LEGACY LIVES — LAMINATED	3.50
28	**THERE'S A NEW DAY COMING — UNLAMINATED	2.00
2801	THERE'S A NEW DAY COMING — LAMINATED	3.50
29	**WALKING IN HIS LIGHT — UNLAMINATED	2.00
2901	WALKING IN HIS LIGHT — LAMINATED	3.50
30	WHAT MANNER OF MEN — UNLAMINATED	5.00
3001	WHAT MANNER OF MEN — LAMINATED	6.50
31	WHAT MANNER OF WOMAN — UNLAMINATED	5.00
3101	WHAT MANNER OF WOMAN — LAMINATED	10.00
32	*WHO ARE WE — UNLAMINATED	2.00
3201	WHO ARE WE — LAMINATED	3.50
33	**YESTERDAY HAS LEFT YOU FOREVER — UNLAMINATED	2.00
3301	YESTERDAY HAS LEFT YOU FOREVER — LAMINATED	3.50
ITEM	**BUILDING DREAMS POSTERS**	PRICE
5881	PROCEDURAL CHART - LAMINATED [indicate title of chart]	10.00
5882	PROCEDURAL CHART - UNLAMINATED [indicate title of chart]	5.00
5811	A PARENT'S VISION - LAMINATED	3.50
5812	A PARENT'S VISION - UNLAMINATED	2.00
5821	WHAT I WON'T DO FOR MY FRIENDS - LAMINATED	3.50
5822	WHAT I WON'T DO FOR MY FRIENDS - UNLAMINATED	2.00
5831	THE AFFIRMATION OF POSSIBILITIES - LAMINATED	3.50
5832	THE AFFIRMATION OF POSSIBILITIES - UNLAMINATED	2.00
5841	DREAM-BUILDER'S CODE OF CONDUCT - LAMINATED	3.50
5842	DREAM-BUILDER'S CODE OF CONDUCT - UNLAMINATED	2.00
5851	DREAM-BUILDER'S AFFIRMATION ALPHABET - LAMINATED	3.50
5852	DREAM-BUILDER'S AFFIRMATION ALPHABET - UNLAMIN.	2.00
5861	DREAM-BUILDER'S AFFIRMATION - LAMINATED	3.50
5862	DREAM-BUILDER'S AFFIRMATION - UNLAMINATED	2.00

Rising Sun Publishing – Product Order Form

How to order by mail

Enter the item number, description, corresponding price, and quantity for each selection (e.g., #1501, Laminated Don't Quit poster, $3.50/ea.) and compute the total for that item. Shipping is 10% of the total (e.g., total order of $200.00 x .10 = $20.00 total shipping). **Allow two weeks for processing.**

Item #	Description **[Please Print]**	Unit Price	X Quantity	= Total

METHOD OF PAYMENT

❏ A check (payable to Rising Sun Publishing) is attached
❏ A purchase order is attached, P.O. # _____
❏ Charge my ❏ Visa ❏ Mastercard ❏ American Express

Account Number _____ Expiration Date _____

Signature (required for credit card purchases) _____

SUBTOTAL $_____

Georgia residents add 6% Sales Tax _____

Handling $ 3.50

Shipping (Subtotal x 10%) _____

DATE: _____ TOTAL $_____

✉ Mail to:
RISING SUN PUBLISHING
P.O. Box 70906
Marietta, GA 30007-0906

Phone toll-free: **1-800-524-2813**
FAX: **1-770-587-0862**

SHIP TO *(PLEASE PRINT)* **[Must be same as billing address for credit card purchases]:**
NAME _____
ADDRESS _____
CITY _____ STATE _____ ZIP _____
DAY PHONE (____) _____ EVE PHONE (____) _____